Where the Sun Don't Shine and the Shadows Don't Play

Where the Sun Don't Shine and the Shadows Don't Play

(Growing up with an Obsessive-Compulsive Hoarder)

Frances Boudreaux

iUniverse, Inc.
Bloomington

Where the Sun Don't Shine and the Shadows Don't Play
(Growing up with an Obsessive-Compulsive Hoarder)

iUniverse books may be ordered through booksellers or by contacting:

iUniverse
1663 Liberty Drive
Bloomington, IN 47403
www.iuniverse.com
1-800-Authors (1-800-288-4677)

ISBN: 978-1-4620-3447-5 (pbk)
ISBN: 978-1-4620-3448-2 (ebk)

Library of Congress Control Number: 2011910771

Printed in the United States of America

iUniverse rev. date: 07/15/2011

To Ken,
for hanging in there with his technologically
challenged wife

My mother and father, Christine and Pat O'Neal—March 1951

CONTENTS

Preface

I remember Mama . . . scrubbing me in a number three, galvanized washtub until I thought my stinging skin would come off on the washrag saturated with Ivory soap.

Why was she so mad at me? What did I do?

I remember Mama adding extra water to the washing machine.

"Why are you doing that?" I asked.

"Because it won't 'rench' [rinse] them clean if I don't," she answered. "Go on, get out of here, stop askin' me all them questions!"

I remember Mama rinsing dishes with water so hot her stubby fingers and hands were blood red. Once rinsed, the dishes would be stacked so high that we wondered how they could stay positioned for days and weeks, roaches crawling over and under them, without ever toppling down.

Shaking off the memories, I pick up the photo album, covered with a dingy, country-rose-patterned fabric, that I made for Mama back in my "earth mother" days. I had retrieved it from under a pile of boxes, pillows, clothing, magazines, and books in my mother's home. I open the eyelet-edged cover and there on the first, yellowed, cellophane page is a fading, umber-tinted, Kodak print of the two people who gave me life.

They sit close together on a chintz-covered sofa. Ancient, Victorian-print wallpaper serves as a backdrop. Daddy has his right leg jauntily crossed over his left. The cuff of his khakis is hiked up, Andy Griffith-style, as if he hadn't a concern in the world. Mama has cocked her left arm casually over Daddy's right shoulder. Her creamy-skinned hand possessively cradles his collarbone. They both appear to be wearing dark tops. Daddy's button-down, long-sleeved dress shirt is open at the neck, revealing the small, white triangle of his cotton undershirt. Mama is wearing a short-sleeved sweater tucked into a tan, pencil skirt with a flared hem. Her right arm lies in her lap slightly camouflaging a bulge in her lower belly. What great shoes she wore, two-toned, high-strapped, open-toed, high-heeled sandals! They seem so relaxed, so alive, so vibrant. So what happened?

Suddenly, the questions of a lifetime ping-pong inside my head. Why did we live as we did? Why did Mama have to be the way she was? How could one person so outrageously affect the lives of five other people? I realized a long time ago that the answers to those questions would not come for me. The fire of them does not burn so terribly in my mind and heart as it once did. Occasionally, they will rekindle and flare a bit, causing me great sadness. I can only hope now that through my all-too-human words I can assist someone who may be suffering silently.

My intention in writing this book is to share in order to enlighten others. It is not to be just another tell-all from a member of a dysfunctional family. For years, I have mulled over and considered constructive ways to impart my family's story. My hope is that others can take something of value from it.

On October 18, 2004, I happened to catch an episode of *Oprah* that focused on people who are household slobs. It was fascinating and painful for me to see a woman named Carol, who was so poised, so well groomed, and who patiently sat while English cleaning experts raked her over the coals because of the disgusting condition of her home. Videos of the interior of her home appeared. The audience gasped at the images of piles of clothing, rotting or long-petrified remnants of food, dog feces filling the bathroom, and all the other examples that seemed meant to shame her for her sloppy housekeeping.

I completely surprised myself at my reaction. Instead of disbelief and disgust (as many of the audience members and even Oprah voiced early on), I instantly empathized with Carol. I also knew that if the people in the audience had been able to see what I had seen over the years, their disbelief would have left them even more open-mouthed and wondering. Carol had nothing on my mama!

Immediately, I recognized Carol's condition. My mother, with whom I rarely empathized through the years, suffered the same condition.

I could see what lay under this woman's carefully constructed mask of deception as to the real nature of her tortuous pain. Carol became the underdog I wanted to champion because she seemed to be reaching out for some sort of help; my mother never did.

All the years of pain, all the years of blame and shame, came back as I watched the program and remembered how I used to think that no one would or could ever understand how it was to live in such a way. I grew up never being able to invite friends from school into my home because I was too embarrassed to explain why there was a mountain of clothes in our living room, which rose six feet high. I also couldn't explain why my mother wouldn't let anyone in our family dispose of those clothes. I couldn't risk having friends look at me with contempt or pity because there were no available chairs for them to sit in. I couldn't take the risk that they might have asked me why I didn't have a bedroom or any space in our home that my mother had not occupied with useless stuff.

My mother's obsessive need to hoard created an unhealthy environment. The dust, mold, and mildew along with vast armies of roaches, rats, and their filthy droppings were what my family had to contend with daily. Spiders and other insects infiltrated the piles and piles of clutter, trash, and debris throughout our house. She could not throw anything away and eventually those things came close to destroying her as her condition deteriorated.

A woman who had grown up poor, unschooled, and neglected created that environment slowly, over many years. Eventually, I had to seek help in order to take the steps necessary to persuade her to move into a nursing home.

This is a case study of one woman's journey into the dark recesses of mental illness—specifically, obsessive-compulsive hoarding—as seen from a familial perspective. I was an adult before I was able to completely and openly share with anyone the painful secret my family kept hidden. Growing up in isolation from others in our small community and from many family members was difficult. However, it did afford my father, my siblings, and me an opportunity to be close to and supportive of one another. Mama would never discuss her illness for what it was or even admit she had an unusual problem. If any one of us asked why she wanted to keep bringing so much junk into the house, she would ignore us. She rapidly changed the subject or shut us up by griping about our shortcomings. She sufficed it to say, "My nerves are bad."

I have seen firsthand the impact of mental illness, not only in my personal history, but also in the small area of the world I inhabit. For many years I have served as an advocate for battered women and children, victims of sexual assault, and for the homeless, some who suffer with mental illnesses and substance abuse issues.

When I contemplate (in my most unscientific manner) the numbers of individuals suffering in this country and around the world, I would hope my words and my very small voice might open genuine dialogue about the mental health care system we currently employ. While most practitioners of public mental health do as good a job as they can, they often face the daunting task of seeing an endless number of individuals. They have limited time to get to the real heart of a person's problems.

The picture becomes even more complicated when factoring in a person like my mother. Mental illness, such as the kind she suffered, is much harder to discern or diagnose if a practitioner sees an incomplete picture of the conditions under which the person exists on a daily basis. (My mother received no official diagnosis of OCD by a certified clinician. That diagnosis is one I gave her after vainly searching for answers and never getting them.) Unfortunately, due to the very nature of her condition, she manipulated the clinicians who saw her over the course of her adult life into believing that her illness was schizophrenia (undifferentiated type) and depression only. They knew Mama had suffered losses that were important to her, but she never disclosed to them or anyone else her overwhelming compulsions and obsessions. Nor did they ever address (with us) her extreme narcissism. Her self-possession was so intense, it bordered on the pathological.

Her self-preservation and needs were always paramount in her thought processes. I do not remember her genuinely considering another person's needs or feelings above her own. That statement is not an exaggeration based on a daughter's disenchantment with her mother. It is frightening to contemplate that someone possesses absolutely no regard for another human.

Perhaps there may never have been an opportunity to assess my mother both psychologically and physically because we were poor and didn't have medical insurance. My father did try early on to get the doctors at the state-run mental health facility to see firsthand the way our family had to live. Unfortunately, they assumed my dad was exaggerating and of course they did not have the time or the capacity to do an in-home study that would have verified the truth.

The evil, insidious nature of obsessive-compulsive disorder not only has a chokehold on the individual who suffers with it, but also on the family and others who might cross the sufferer's path. The daily walk is fraught with pitfalls of frustration as well as feelings of apathy, guilt, shame, impotence, and ultimately failure to know how to be in relationship with the sufferer. Do you "love the sinner and hate the sin?"

As a social worker friend of mine once said, "The best advice I can give to a family dealing with OCD is to run like hell!" It sometimes saddens me to say that I did exactly that. After years of frustration, anger, and just wanting the answer to "why," I made the decision to back away. It was not an easy decision to make. Spiritually and morally, I thought I had to "see about my mama." After all, societal views about the virtues of motherhood are such that an individual seems to commit an awful crime, particularly in the South, if she does not take care of her "poor mama." "She cain't hep it," as they might say.

Mental health professionals have varying views on obsessive-compulsive personality disorder, with hoarding viewed as a subset or symptom of OCD. Some experts see obsessive-compulsive disorder as one of perfectionism, inflexibility, and/or problems associated with chronic disorganization. Still others see it as a neurological defect of the brain with an imbalance of hormones, particularly the serotonin levels, being an underlying cause.

Hoarding is thought to be rare in the general population, but nobody is sure how rare it is because there have been no general studies done. Although hoarding is not one of the diagnostic criteria of OCD, about 25–30 percent of those patients show significant hoarding compulsions, according to Zsuzsa Meszaros, MD, PhD, and Walter A. Brown, MD ("The Perils of Compulsive Hoarding and How to Intervene," *Psychiatric Times*, May 31, 2006).

The *Diagnostic and Statistical Manual of Mental Disorders*, 4th ed, (Arlington, VA: American Psychiatric Association, 1994), 672–73, describes obsessive-compulsive personality disorder as "a pervasive pattern of preoccupation with orderliness, perfectionism, and mental and interpersonal control, at the expense of flexibility, openness, and efficiency, beginning by early adulthood and present in a variety of contexts, as indicated by four (or more) of the following:

- is preoccupied with details, rules, lists, order, organization, or schedules to the extent that the major point of the activity is lost
- shows perfectionism that interferes with task completion (e.g., is unable to complete a project because his or her own overly strict standards are not met)

- is excessively devoted to work and productivity to the exclusion of leisure activities and friendships (not accounted for by obvious economic necessity)
- is overly conscientious, scrupulous, and inflexible about matters of morality, ethics, or values (not accounted for by cultural or religious identification)
- is unable to discard worn-out or worthless objects even when they have no sentimental value
- is reluctant to delegate tasks or to work with others unless they submit to exactly his or her way of doing things
- shows rigidity and stubbornness
- adopts a miserly spending style toward both self and others and the individual may view hoarding money as necessary for future catastrophes"

I would add magical thinking and superstition to this list.

Categorically, when I first saw this list, I thought, *Now wait a minute, not all of that seems to fit my mother.* After careful studying and further research, as well as my family's extensive library of memories associated with the peculiarities of Mama's personality, I knew without a doubt that the definition fit her. I can accept this definition in relation to my mother's personality now, although, at one time I wouldn't have considered that she had any degree of perfectionism about her. It seems paradoxical to say that someone living in deplorable filth whose personal hygiene became nightmarish was considered a perfectionist, but she was. Someone suffering with OCD operates by their own sets of standards based on their own views of what they consider as good or bad. Family members must often cope with someone whose thinking is extraordinarily black and white. Beliefs held by the person are unbending and nonnegotiable.

In his book, *Obsessive-Compulsive Disorders: Treating and Understanding Crippling Habits*, psychotherapist Steven Levenkron sees OCD as "the personality's attempt to reduce anxiety, which may stem from a painful childhood or a genetic tendency toward anxiety that just won't quit" (Levenkron 1991). This simple statement spoke volumes to me: the need to reduce anxiety that just will not quit.

Throughout my childhood and up until Mama died, she exhibited overwhelming anxiety woes. Once she was in a much more controlled environment where someone monitored her, she became less likely to do harm to herself because of how she lived.

Her anxieties became the central frustration that my father, brother, and two sisters had to challenge daily. I say frustration because at times it was next to impossible to convince Mama that someone wasn't going to cheat her.

She would always say, "Count that money; she [the bank teller] might try to beat [cheat] me out of some."

We would tell her the house wasn't going to burn down and that none of us left the stove on. However, she always said, "Go back and check that burner before we leave."

The endless arguments, accusations, and abuse she inflicted on every one of us was her way of telling us that she was anxious and fearful about some unknown thing, something that overwhelmed her daily. We didn't comprehend or understand, and she certainly never told any of us what those compulsive thoughts and obsessions that drove her might have been.

We could only see her behavior as detrimental to our existence. Day-to-day living was a minefield of potential situations for outlandish, obnoxious, or rude behavior, petty arguments, or screaming matches with or from Mama in an overall atmosphere of domestic discord. Her seemingly nonsensical worries and histrionics over the most mundane occurrences kept every one of us off-kilter at times, and over the years, this behavior took its toll on us by compounding our own worries and fears.

We learned to "live around" the episodes the same way a spouse or intimate partner does in a case of domestic violence, which is in essence the legal definition of how we did live. That hypervigilant atmosphere of living as though we were walking on eggshells or waiting for something bad to happen robbed my family of joy and peace of mind.

My mother was hard and coarse and occasionally loud and vulgar. The world she had known seemed to me to reflect some of the things she described, like the backwoods places she had seen where she said they had to "pipe in sunshine."

Sometimes she threatened those of us who got in her way with the act of putting her foot "where the sun don't shine," which embarrassingly translated to me that we were all up the ass of chaos and distortion. This allusion of an absence of light surfaced and resurfaced throughout my turbulent relationship with Mama. She seemed most at home when the shadows were thick, clingy, and foreboding. I, on the other hand, longed for and coveted living in an environment that was peacefully clean, where the shadows playfully danced over clear surfaces.

I fully believe we survived so that we could share what we learned in order to assist others. We did have many blessings granted to us. Those blessings were rooted in the knowledge that our father, Pat O'Neal, unconditionally loved us.

I have come to believe that all those old family secrets from the '40s, '50s, and '60s are why there are so many individuals presently seeking or in need of therapy. Many, many people who grew up in those years never received adequate modeling or the skills needed to be in an intimate relationship or to raise children, two of the most important things a person could ever do as an adult.

I suppose some could look at all of this and say, "Why bother? So what? What's the point of recording a family's time together?" The study of psychology explains that the moments from an individual's birth until the age of two determine much about the course of things to come for that individual. The person's environment, socialization, and subsequent development merge in this first 730 days to effect that individual for the rest of his/her life. Those 730 days are not monitored daily by anyone outside of an immediate family circle (and I am not suggesting it should be otherwise).

We presuppose that when a woman and a man join and create a human life they will be responsible for that created life. When the significance of the 730 days is considered, the enormity of what will transpire is overwhelming; yet we as a society accept that parents will "do right" by their offspring. I believe it comes down to our considering that someone who commits atrocities must be sick or crazy, so that we are able to reconcile within ourselves the unthinkable gravity of such acts. The redemptive factor for me has been that I accept and believe that the presence of my father as a positive adult in my life helped me overcome the negative effects of a mother who was not "done right" by the adults in her youth. However, what would have been the repercussions had my father not been present and available?

I have known that at some point in my life, I would need to chronicle the journey my father, my siblings, and

I endured living with an obsessive-compulsive hoarder. For more years than I care to remember, we lived in the shadow of an overwhelming shame and sense of isolation wrought by the keeping of a vicious secret we thought no one would believe. We were a family collectively controlled by a disease so insidious that any attempt to seek help made the seeker appear to be the sick one.

Outsiders could not fathom the depth of despair or the wretchedness of our existence. Even the few family members who were allowed within those walls became complicit. They too could make no sense of why a woman would choose to have her family live in such conditions. They simply chose not to be involved because Christine was obviously "sick" and could not "help it." Everyone outside the immediate family remained silent. No one came together for any sort of productive intervention.

I am the oldest of the four children of Pat and Christine O'Neal. My family's story takes place in the heart of the Deep South, central Louisiana. The burdens of a family are often hidden from the community, especially in small towns or communities. Unfortunately, our legacy has been further tainted by ignorance, illiteracy, and a stubborn need to remain steadfast in a swamp of tradition, which does not allow cycles of family discord to be broken. Too often we're told, "That's just the way it was, so get over it, and go on," and we do, but we just continue to carry that burdensome bag forever. I now share the story of my family, in the tone and the voice of the child I was and the adult I came to be.

Acknowledgments

I would like to thank my sister Janis for being the childhood confidant who helped me persevere and who stood by me growing up. I thank my brother, Oscar, for his humble sincerity and loving support. To my baby sister, Kitty, I am grateful for your honesty and loving encouragement. To my father, Pat O'Neal, I give deep honor and love to the man who encouraged me to learn and to dig deeper when I didn't understand. To my mother, Christine, I wish you could have known your children differently.

I especially thank Brenda Beckerdite, who offered early encouragement, constructive suggestions, insight, and honesty. To my dear friends Rebecca Williams and Tammy George, I am grateful for your honest reading and encouragement. I am grateful for the love and positive encouragement of my in-laws, Claudia and Rick Larriviere.

I deeply appreciate the professional assistance offered by Richard Sharkey and am thankful for his encouragement. To Patricia Powell, I offer gratitude for your knowledge, assistance, and sisterly advice. To Kathy Gunn, I am forever indebted to you and am in awe of your skill.

To my children, Courtney, Patrick, and Colleen, I give my love and gratitude for your support. To my stepchildren,

Kari, Adam, and Kevin, I offer my love and thanks for your encouragement.

I cannot adequately thank my husband, Ken, for the patience, love, and encouragement he gave me during this process of trying to tell my story.

Chapter 1

A Stray Mama Cat and Her Kittens

I saw two decidedly different views of motherhood as I was growing up. Both of my parents grew up without the presence of their biological fathers. My mother's mother, Lavinia, and my father's mother, Linnie, were both financially poor and had to scrape to get by. Each of them brought many children into the world, but this is where their similarities ended.

I was ashamed of Mama and her family for many, many years. I suppose some would call that a sin. In trying to sort through the possible reasons for that strong emotion, I have finally concluded that I detested stinginess. I felt that my mother's family represented that spirit. I do know what it is like to grow up poor, but I didn't experience the kind of financial poverty and the extreme poverty of the human mind and spirit that seemed to be characteristic of some of my mother's family. I am grateful that I didn't have to know that way of life, but my mother did, and her blood courses through my veins.

I sometimes feel within myself the distinction between the two families. I am hard-pressed to know if the

1

characteristics that I possess, the ones I feel good about, are within me because I was nurtured on my father's side. When I think of being loved, I think of my father and his family—they cherished children and encouraged them.

The characteristics I don't like feel as though they come from some darker place, something I saw in my mother. So is it nature or nurture? I know that she was not cherished; she was not encouraged. Sadness envelops me when I think about what she might have been or what she might have achieved had someone taken the time to love and cherish her when she was a little girl.

My mother's name was Christine. It seemed to me that her mama and daddy didn't think enough of her to give her a middle name. Christine Hines, "Chrissie," was the unfinished one, the little girl who was damaged goods and sold to the darkness of neglect and abuse. I would like to have seen pictures of her as a child to see what story her eyes told, but there are none to be found.

I believe my mother suffered from high anxiety all of her life. She was nervous about everything.

"Did you leave the back door open?"

"Go see if I turned the burner on the stove off."

When I hear myself say similar things, I know that she infused me with that same anxiety. It has taken me a number of years to come close to understanding even a minute amount of what may have motivated her and what may have been at the core of the illness she suffered. This disorder had a terrible chokehold on her and in turn greatly affected my family and me.

Mama was the youngest daughter of the nine children of Lavinia Martin Hines Carrington Lasyone, who outlived her three husbands. "Lavinyer" (as so many people pronounced her name) was a spitfire, razor-toting, hate-filled, spite-filled woman. I can only remember my grandmother as being mean and contrary. I only have vague clues as to why she may have behaved the way she did.

Looking now at the black-and-white photograph I have of Maw Maw Lavinia as an adult, sitting calmly posed in the formal way of photographers of the '60s, made in some long-forgotten Alexandria, Louisiana, portrait studio, I am inclined to wonder what was so imposing and threatening about her. I intently study the woman who is sitting rather uncomfortably with her head slightly cocked (again, a device used by photography studios) wearing dark-rimmed glasses, perhaps in her late fifties. It is obvious that her dentures were ill fitted, causing her smile to appear fake. Her hands are clasped in a staged, humble pose. Was this the way she wanted her family to remember her? On the other hand, was this the way she wanted other people to see her?

My mother didn't speak fondly of her mother or seem to hold her with a great deal of regard, although they spoke by phone almost daily. There were no terms of endearment or physical demonstrations of love and affection or any affirming statements exchanged between them. From my childish perspective, Maw Maw Lavinia was not a woman easy to like or to be close to because she didn't seem to like anyone or to be close to anyone. Although my siblings and I were to spend a great deal of time around her as children, we were never able to develop a strong bond with her. At best, she tolerated us.

Maw Maw Lavinia was of French descent. According to Mama, she was a "Coonass," although she didn't have the Cajun accent of someone who is known by that popular term. This derogatory name, commonly applied to folks of French heritage in Louisiana, said all there was to say for many people. This one word is the way some Louisianans refer to individuals also known as Cajuns. It becomes a convenient, stereotypical name applied to someone who might otherwise be characterized as fiery, excitable, mean-tempered, eccentric, or even crazy. Unfortunately, at times Maw Maw Lavinia could be all these things and more.

I have asked myself repeatedly, what happened back then? What in the world happened to Maw Maw Lavinia? Was she physically, emotionally, or sexually abused so that she was robbed of her soul? Did the extreme poverty she endured force an ancient tribal need to survive to throb intensely through the core of her being? Additionally, was that why she was steered later to make decisions that led her to offer her children's innocence as a sacrifice upon some unholy altar?

A sad, tragic occurrence may have shaped my grandmother Lavinia's personality. She was orphaned as an infant when her parents and a sibling were killed in a house fire. She was taken in and raised by an unknown family in the rural city of Winnfield, in Winn Parish in northeast Louisiana. This is the area known as the birthplace of the infamous politically dynastic Long family. The place Paul Newman (who starred in the movie *Blaze* about Huey Long's younger brother "Uncle Earl") even today is greeted with a "Welcome, Paul Newman" sign on the side of an old building as you enter the city along US 167.

I believe that being poor and undereducated in the early part of the twentieth century, in the South, had to have been a miserable place to be. I surmise that there was no process made available to Maw Maw Lavinia to work out her grief and terror over losing her family in such a horrific fashion. I never knew that part of her history until recently. That revelation was shocking because none of the family ever talked about it when I was a child. Why didn't they? It was not a shameful thing. Maybe I would have looked at her differently, more empathetically, had I known she had grown up without her parents.

As a matter of course, there weren't many stories shared in Mama's family—no passing of family history to illuminate the trials and tribulations they might have endured and certainly no mention of moments that were joyous or celebratory. Maybe the nature of their existence was something they all wanted to leave behind, especially Maw Maw Lavinia.

Most likely, she was pushed into marriage as a very young girl. Probably this was a convenient way for the family who took her in to be relieved of another mouth to feed. Her first marriage may have been one of convenience. Maw Maw Lavinia probably didn't ever have a chance to learn what trust, communication, and, most importantly, love was about. It seemed that she could never be happy or at peace, no matter where she went. She spent much of her life moving around, seeking some illusory form of fulfillment.

I don't know much about my grandmother's first husband, my biological grandfather. Nor do I know how they came to be together. My speculations about him intensified when I learned that Francis "Pick" Hines was twenty-seven years older than Maw Maw Lavinia. She was eighteen when they married in Winnfield on August 6, 1919. As I searched for clues about my maternal grandmother's past, I felt such sadness upon discovering their marriage certificate in the Winnfield courthouse. The courthouse records listed her parents, Alice and Jim Martin, as "dead" in the spaces designated for residence.

Pick Hines had earned a living as a sawmill worker. He suffered from diabetes and due to complications of the disease, had to have one of his legs amputated. My mother thought that his nickname probably came from the fact that he was an amputee. At the time of my mother's birth on May 7,

1935, the two of them were living in Goldonna, Louisiana. This community lies in a rural portion of Natchitoches Parish in the north central part of the state. My mother referred to the area as being up in "the farming country."

This fertile land north of Alexandria was replete with plantations and farms, which were cotton-producing strongholds during the Civil War. The parish is beautiful, with pastoral settings and magnificently regal orchards of pecan trees that grow everywhere. It is alive with the history of a diverse population. Mama's recollections to us of the area weren't about its beauty or history, but rather the harshness of her life there. As a child, I pictured Goldonna as a dusty, little town of illiterate, poor, white people.

Mama didn't talk very much about her father. She didn't say what he might have meant to her and her brothers and sisters. It almost seemed as if he never existed. I suppose that essentially he didn't. The man left not much of a story for anyone to carry on. My mother was a small child when Hines's diabetes worsened, causing him to be seriously ill. Later, he was transported to Shreveport for hospitalization. He died there.

New troubles brewed for my grandmother and her children after Hines died. Apparently, my grandfather had been married before and had other children. According to Mama, somehow Hines's first family was able to stake claim to his compensatory death benefits after he died, leaving Maw Maw Lavinia with very little except bitter feelings. My mother was five years old at the time. I can't imagine what it must have been like for my grandmother to have so many children, no money (except what was earned by working in the fields), and no family to turn to.

Mama's siblings were Hayward, Mary Alice, Frank, Claudie, Jettie Mae, Earl and Robert Hines, and Jesse Patrick Carrington. Whisperings within the family revealed an allegation that Maw Maw Lavinia gave Earl and Robert (the youngest sons carrying the Hines name) away as toddlers. Their oldest sister, Mary Alice, virtually raised the two boys with the help of her husband, Jeff Malone. Robert and Earl were gentle spirited; both became upstanding, family-oriented men.

Rumor also has it that these two sons may have been fathered by Jeff Malone, who was considerably older than my aunt Mary Alice. That story has circulated for a very long time, but no one will refute or verify whether my grandmother Lavinia had a sexual relationship with Jeff Malone. It is also puzzling as to why her daughter Mary Alice came to be with him. If the story is true, Aunt Mary Alice wasn't only half sister to her brothers, but their stepaunt and stepmother as well. Maw Maw Lavinia must have given birth to her first child, Hayward, and her first daughter, Mary Alice, early in her marriage to Pick Hines for Aunt Mary Alice to be old enough to become a mother figure to her younger brothers.

Like a stray mama cat moving its kittens, Maw Maw Lavinia moved her large brood many times. After Hines's death and quite possibly after she married Pat Carrington, she and the children left Goldonna and headed south to central Louisiana, about an hour and a half away. My mother indicated that the family had lived along the banks of Little River in east Grant Parish (about twenty-five miles north of Pineville) at some time, in or around a community known as Cotton Island. This was a kind of no-man's-land of outlaws and ne'er-do-wells. There they would have encountered other undereducated, working poor. The folks who lived there would have fished the river for catfish, bream, and crappie and hunted the land where game, such as deer, ducks, and squirrels, was plentiful.

This wasn't a place for children. I cringe when I think about the story my aunt Jettie told her children. She was down by the water, unattended, when she was bitten by a cottonmouth water moccasin (one of the deadliest snakes in the South). An old black man came upon the scene and managed to pull the snake off her leg. Aunt Jettie said he sucked some of the venom out of the wound before he carried her home. The kind old man advised my grandmother to take her little girl to the hospital, but Maw Maw Lavinia told him they couldn't do that. Aunt Jettie said they treated her at home by packing the bite with rags soaked in coal oil. She was terribly sick for days. I can imagine that there were many other tales similar to that one—more terrible things they may have witnessed or been party to.

Eventually, Maw Maw Lavinia moved to Pineville, Louisiana. It sits on the east side of the Red River directly across from Alexandria, the largest city in the central region of the state. Once in Pineville, they made their way to Wardville, an economically depressed neighborhood on the eastern outskirts of the city.

Because Maw Maw Lavinia moved frequently, she probably lived in every available rental house in the Alexandria/Pineville area over the course of her lifetime. I couldn't begin to remember the number of houses she lived in when I was a child. Maybe she never felt as though she belonged anywhere. Her wandering may have been her way of trying to find some place to take root. Because they were poor, this may have been the lot cast for herself and her offspring. She moved as often as twice in a single month. Sometimes she lived in the same rental house multiple times.

Many of the houses she lived in were near the levee of the muddy, fast-flowing currents of the Red River that separates Pineville and Alexandria. She usually rented in the poorer sections of those cities. Often, there was a colorful mix of characters; Maw Maw Lavinia could tell you everything about her neighbors and then some. Some type of drama was always taking place. If situations became too intense or too heated, she'd pack up and move. Like a gypsy, she would sometimes move overnight if the mood struck her. This nomadic existence never lent itself to developing a stable home.

As older siblings sometimes did, two of my uncles, Hayward and Frank, looked for logging work in the area. The logging industry has been a staple of the economy on the north side of the Red River for many years. Pulpwood loggers, haulers, and sawmill workers had a rough life. They had to contend with extremes of stifling, oppressively humid heat in the summer and wet, bitter-cold winters. This was backbreaking work from sunup to sundown. Their hard physical labor consisting of cutting, sawing, and lifting felled trees was a demanding way to earn a living.

Frank was just two weeks shy of his seventeenth birthday when he was involved in a horrific accident at the north Rapides Parish sawmill. He tried to prime an engine carburetor with gasoline. A random spark ignited the gasoline, which then exploded in his face. Frank's entire body was engulfed in flames as he ran from the scene. Because Frank panicked, Uncle Hayward wasn't able to stop him quickly enough to put out the flames. Frank died because he was burned over 80 percent of his body. Mama said he wore mismatched socks to work the day he died and that was the reason he was killed. This was the type of reasoning used in her family to explain a tragic life occurrence.

That story resonated with me so much that even now, when folding clothes, I am still compelled to put socks together that match! There didn't seem to be a great deal of horror or sadness associated with his death. The telling of his demise was almost matter-of-fact. More than anything, it revealed to me the superstitious nature of Mama's family and their lack of compassion for one another. It left a resounding impression on me that you don't take chances with anything, even your selection of socks.

The picture I had of my mother's childhood was that it had been a mean, hardscrabble life. Maw Maw Lavinia personified that life; it showed in the lines of her face and her pinched lips. There was a perpetual scowl on her face and a suspicious sharpness in her eyes as she gazed out from behind the thick lenses of her glasses. She took an adversarial stance with those she encountered, as if to say, "I'll get you before you can get me." This attitude toward life was largely adopted by my mother and her sisters. They showed no prejudice in who they slighted or backstabbed or who they manipulated to get what they wanted. Few of them trusted anyone; they were clannish and wary. Like a pack of stray dogs, they would slowly circle a new person who came into their midst, sizing him up before developing a relationship with him.

Maw Maw Lavinia told her children of her days of picking cotton, dragging the sacks behind as she slowly filled them. As she toiled in the sweltering humidity of the Louisiana farm country, she would leave her infant children on a quilt pallet with a "sugar tit" to pacify them. (This was a piece of cloth filled with a wad of sugar, knotted with string, and given to babies to gnaw on.)

The brutal work, rough times, and poor living conditions hardened this small woman to the core. Maw Maw Lavinia would pin a cloth sack inside her brassiere to hide her money from her own family. Like a spiteful child, her hiding and hoarding of possessions was a way of being. She stingily hid any love for all but one of her children, her youngest son, Jesse Patrick. Maw Maw Lavinia dominated through manipulation and guilt-ridden demands. Her children were expected to do for her, not the other way around. The lessons they learned from her were how to be manipulative and mean spirited. Not every one of them adopted her way of being, especially the sons, but they were surely marked in some way by her usually devious behavior.

Maw Maw Lavinia's second husband, Pat Carrington, was also older than she was. He and his brother, Ike, moved in and became part of the large family. Pat and Ike were alcoholics. Although I have no substantial recollection of either of them, I do recall the family saying that Pat and Ike were notorious for their drinking. Pat in particular "laid up drunk" most of the time. My grandmother defended his behavior. This became a cause of disagreement between her and her Hines sons.

After becoming adults, Robert and Earl had very little to do with their mother. After all, she had thrown them away and now she was with a man who was mean-spirited and a drunkard as well! As a small child, I vaguely remember a visit in her home at another rental house that had high ceilings and large rooms. I opened a bedroom door and saw Pat in his bed. I don't know if he was drunk or sick, but I was quickly told not to bother him. In that dimly lit room, I saw a pint whiskey bottle near the bed, which the adults told me was his toddy. Apparently, he had combined the whiskey with honey and lemon to give it the appearance of being medicinal. My grandmother was a teetotaler, but she tolerated Pat's drinking and made excuses for him, although she looked derisively on anyone else who drank.

Pat Carrington was considered mean and hateful by the family. Maw Maw Lavinia probably saw a means to an end when she decided to marry him. He drew some sort of government pension; most likely, he had been in the military and received veteran's benefits, so she didn't have to worry about how she would live. Jesse Patrick was the only child of that union and my grandmother's favorite. He was the one she doted on and sent to parochial elementary school.

Evidently, Pat Carrington was the husband my grandmother Lavinia most clung to and thought of as her only true spouse. His name was brought up in many adult conversations I overheard, even after his death. There was a certain amount of mystery around him. This made me wonder how he might have affected the lives of the children.

By happenstance, as an adult, I encountered a woman who came from Goldonna who knew my mother's family. I'm sure I surprised this perfect stranger with an unusual question after a brief and casual conversation regarding her recollections of my mother's family. With no emotion, I asked her if something had happened to my mother when she was a child. The woman asked what I meant. I told her I didn't know, but was it possible that my mother had been hurt when she was a little girl.

In a polite, kind, and sweetly Southern voice, she said, "Honey, I don't hardly know you and I wouldn't want to hurt your feelings."

My heart thumped loudly in my ears as I calmly told her that I wouldn't be surprised or offended by anything she shared with me. At that time, I worked as an advocate for battered women, children, and victims of sexual assault with a nonprofit agency. I was more than familiar with horrifying things that happened in families.

After all my years of "why" questions about my mother's mental health, I had reached a tiny measure of peace by realizing that most likely she had been some kind of victim as a child. The woman paused again. Finally, she said that there had been some talk in the community that Pat Carrington had raped my mother when she was twelve years old. That information, although an allegation, was startling to me.

If the revelation was accurate, it could explain much about my mother's behavior on many levels. I believe that perhaps my grandmother may have known what happened to my mother and then covered it up. By doing so, she invalidated my mother and crippled her emotionally. Although Mama had physically developed at an early age, I don't believe she ever emotionally matured beyond the age of twelve.

Pat Carrington died when I was a small child and it wasn't very long before my grandmother married again.

My grandmother Lavinia's last husband was Lee Lasyone, a retired barber. He too had been an alcoholic, but a recovering one when she married him. Lee hailed from the city of Colfax in Grant Parish. He was an eccentric old fart who always dressed like a throwback to his perception of a genteel South.

Lee was fastidious and well groomed. He liked to wear a suit jacket, dress shirt, string tie, and felt hat. I remember how he would come out of the bathroom in dress khakis and a "wife-beater" undershirt, with his suspenders hanging down to his knees, and his ever-present fedora. He liked to get slicked-up before he went anywhere.

Lee presented himself as an educated man who was smarter and more socially prominent than any one of us was. The time he spent as a successful businessman and his military veteran status seemed to give him special influence over other folks. I only remember him as obnoxious, especially when he would involve himself in outlandish arguments with store clerks or anyone he thought beneath his intelligence. Maw Maw Lavinia demanded that we show him respect.

My sister Janis and I often used the '60s term of being creeped-out by his lecherous stares and lascivious innuendoes. During our midteen years, we often stayed at Maw Maw Lavinia's house, so there was no way to avoid the old man. When Lee saw a pretty girl, he made mumbling utterances in a low voice, so that we couldn't hear him. He sometimes remarked about particular clothes Janis and I might wear or sneaked a pinch occasionally. He never made any overt approaches to either of us, but we were intuitively careful around him all the same.

Lee usually had some old pickup that he drove like the proverbial bat out of hell. He was a shrunken, hunched-over, old man in glasses terrorizing the highways! He would embarrass Janis and me so much we would hide on the floorboard, fearful we might see someone we knew. Many times, he narrowly missed hapless motorists as he roared past, flinging nasty curses their way, ignoring the flipped middle fingers they jabbed out at him from half-opened car windows.

Both he and my grandmother were up in age at the time of their marriage so no children came of their union. Mama tolerated him and he tolerated Mama. I believe he came closest to being a type of father figure in her eyes because she deferred to him much of the time. She thought Lee Lasyone had money and she courted those with money. It was in her best interest to stay on his good side. Although she wouldn't speak well of him in our home, she spoke kindly to him at my grandmother's house. My mother had a reputation of being docile and sweet within her family.

My siblings and I visited in Maw Maw Lavinia's home quite often during the time she was married to Lee because Mama was receiving mental health treatment and she had to have a place to leave us. Most often, we had the feeling that we weren't welcome. She wagged her finger in our faces and griped at us if we meddled with her things or went into her refrigerator. She was very particular about Lee's belongings and continually told us that his things were off-limits to us.

She would say, "Don't mess with that apple butter, 'cause Lee likes to have that with his biscuits!"

The only time she asked for Janis and me to come stay with her was when she wanted ironing or cleaning done. She paid us ten cents apiece to iron Lee's shirts.

My maternal grandmother pitted her children against each other. Maw Maw Lavinia was forever stirring the pot, carrying vicious tales back and forth via telephone or in person. (Gossip and innuendo were the keystones for the women of this family. The men seemed not to adopt the behavior.) The bickering, the arguments, and the cursing that took place between family members were mind numbing and frustrating.

The mother/daughter relationships between Maw Maw Lavinia and her four daughters were brutal. Tension, animosity, and jealousy were continually at play in their lives. They never expressed genuine regard for one another. Instead, they would fake responses. For instance, if one sister acquired something new, the others feigned halfhearted congratulations to her face. As soon as they got back to their own homes, the telephone lines were burning with their put-downs of that particular sister. Mama was most often singled out as the object of their envy and backstabbing because my father was respectful of her. He had a good job early in their marriage and had provided her with a decent home.

Maw Maw Lavinia was thick in the middle of the family squabbles and many times the instigator of it. If she didn't like someone or didn't agree with him or her, it was damn well expected that she would "cuss" a person out in rapid order. Her temper was widely known and feared even though she was slight in stature and build. She wasn't embarrassed to confront anyone.

My grandmother didn't care much for cooking. I have no memory of sitting down as a family at her house and having a meal. She cooked foods with seasonings like salt pork and fatback and little else. The first time I ever saw pickled pig's feet was at her house. I was disgusted and shocked by those pink hooves swimming in a big jar of vinegar! The pots of cooked food would stay on the stove, from which you served yourself, if you so desired.

Breakfast there consisted of hard biscuits with salt pork and a can of Steen's thick, black cane syrup to pour over the biscuits. The one pleasant smell in her house was the aroma of freshly brewed, dark, chicory-style coffee. She made it in a little white enamel coffee pot that had a sock-type filter for the dripped brew.

Maw Maw Lavinia's house, wherever that might have been, was always neat and clean; it just wasn't very inviting. My grandmother certainly did nothing to lend an air of hospitality to the setting either.

Maw Maw Lavinia was not a nurturing sort of woman. I don't remember any of her grandchildren sitting on her lap or laughing with her. She was solicitous toward the grandkids whose characteristics were more like hers and her daughters'. When any of us were old enough to engage in gossip and troublemaking, then she would champion that particular grandchild. Because we didn't engage in the behavior, my siblings and I never received even that regard.

She was not loving and giving nor patient and kind. Most of her children, especially the girls, held a fierce loyalty to her, though, and frequently visited in her home.

Their relationships perplexed Daddy and me quite a bit. They never got along, but they were incapable of breaking away from each other. I have come to understand that this is very typical of people in unhealthy relationships. Many of us tend to stick with what we know. It's easier to deal with the familiar, even if it is hurtful, than to explore new ways of being that can seem frightening, even if they can also be liberating. My grandmother had expectancies for her daughters that involved doing her bidding; this allowed her to control whatever situations came along.

Giving her kids an opportunity to obtain a formal education didn't seem to be a priority for Maw Maw Lavinia. Most of them didn't finish high school, with the possible exception of Jesse. My grandmother allowed Mama to drop out of school in the sixth grade. She couldn't read and could barely sign her name. This fact puzzled me for many years because my mother was the youngest daughter. The opportunity to go to school was probably much more available to her than it was to the older kids, but for some reason, Maw Maw Lavinia didn't deem it necessary for my mother to further her education. I now wonder if this may have been another indicator of Pat Carrington's alleged sexual abuse.

I was told by my aunt Jettie that if any of the girls didn't want to go to school on a given day, Maw Maw Lavinia simply allowed that to happen. Rather than go to school, the girls would work in the fields along with their mother. Therefore, Claudie, Jettie, and Mama, the younger daughters, never progressed beyond elementary or junior high. I'm certain Mary Alice didn't go that far either. All of Mama's sisters could read and write to some extent, enough to get by. Only Mama was illiterate.

Their lack of education was my greatest source of shame as a child. Some of Mama's family members spoke out of ignorance and misinformation. This never seemed to bother them, but it embarrassed me terribly. My father had seen this belief system regarding education firsthand. He remembered a saying from his own childhood that seems apt for this situation: "I hain't gonna larn nothin' 'cause my pap didn't know nothin'!"

After I started school, I quickly realized the extent of my mother's illiteracy. My father's cousin, Shirley Rayner, my sister Janis, my brother, Oscar, and I were riding in our family car as Mama drove along the highway very near our home. We stopped at the little country grocery store on the highway so Mama could pick up milk and bread. I looked up at the big sign advertising the specials of the day. A mischievous spell came upon me and for some reason I asked Mama to tell me what the sign said. If the truth were told, I probably knew what it said, and maybe I was testing her.

I was in the backseat with Janis and Oscar, so I leaned forward to make the request. Shirley later told her sister-in-law, Marbeth, that Mama slapped me so hard it made her want to cry. I don't think I ever referred to Mama's inability to read again after that incident. We children learned that Mama expected us to cover for her inability to read. Her standard statement to us was, "I can't make that out, so tell me what it says," as if she was having trouble seeing the printed page. It wasn't something we talked about as a rule. We simply knew that it was a subject best not brought up.

Although Maw Maw Lavinia and Mama talked almost daily, I don't ever remember my mother going to her own mother for helpful or supportive advice or comfort. Most often, she turned to my paternal grandmother, Linnie, and her own older sister, Mary Alice, for guidance. She and her mother would gripe to each other about situations or people or engage in gossip but Mama didn't seem to trust her mother with information that was personal.

I've found it exceedingly odd that my grandmother's sons, as adults, sought some kind of spiritual sustenance, but the daughters didn't. I can't recall any of them going to church or expressing any fundamental beliefs in God or a higher power, which would have been the norm in this part of the South. They would occasionally mouth platitudes or common sayings associated with religion, almost in a superstitious, warding-off-of-bad-luck sort of way. "Oh, Lord" and "Jesus Christ" peppered their conversations, but that was the extent of it.

Maw Maw Lavinia kept Sacred Heart of Jesus pictures hanging around her house that reflected a Roman Catholic sensibility, but I don't recall her practicing that faith. My grandmother remained mean and ornery until only a few years before she died. She started attending a small Baptist church in Wardville, which I believe was the home church of her son Earl and his wife, Linda. The pastor would visit her, which she seemed to enjoy. I couldn't tell if it was genuine or not. Maybe toward the end of her life she felt a need to "get right with God."

Maw Maw Lavinia had a stroke about two years before she died, sometime around 1971. I remember thinking when I visited her that I didn't know her with this new behavior. She was quite docile and gentle, and she smiled more than I had ever witnessed. It was as though I was visiting an imposter. She seemed delicate and it made me uncomfortable because I didn't know how to be in her presence. She talked in the third person as Mama did when she wanted something. With outreached hands she beckoned, "Come see Maw Maw, baby." It was an odd feeling to hear her words.

Although her mother or sisters didn't nurture Mama in a positive way, they did baby and enable her. They treated her as though she was helpless and stupid; "Poor Chrissie" became the mantra they used repeatedly. I now wonder if my mother's alleged rape was covered up in order to protect Pat Carrington and to protect Maw Maw Lavinia from being vilified in public. It is probable that the ensuing guilt felt by Maw Maw Lavinia and the sisters led them to treat Mama as a perpetual cripple. It was as if they wanted to keep her childlike, shielded from the realities of life, and yet still maintain a competitive relationship with her. It was never an even playing field. Someone always wanted the upper hand.

Even as a kid, I discerned that the relationship my mother had with her sisters and her mother was not quite the way it should be. From my perspective, they didn't appear to respect her. They seemed to view her as less than they were, as pathetic. Their attitude was similar to the way some families might hold back a physically or developmentally disabled person. In my family's ignorant bid to protect Mama, they left her wide open to an emotional stunting. She was never able to move forward.

Mama may have inadvertently set this dynamic up herself as a child. She may have been traumatized by her stepfather's alleged sexual abuse. I'm inclined to believe that she experienced many hurtful things in her childhood. Aunt Jettie spoke of some of the abuses that she and her sisters suffered at one time or another, certainly emotional and physical abuse.

Given Mama's uncanny ability to read vulnerability in others, she may have learned that by behaving weak and vulnerable, the older sisters wouldn't get the better of her or get more things than she did. She could gain the unhealthy attention and sympathy that she so desperately craved. This unhealthy style of coping was likely to have been forged when Mama was a child. It worked, so she continued using it. It seemed to me that the adults in her life had failed her.

My mother never learned how to fend for herself because someone constantly rescued her. She became dependent on everyone else to handle the adult situations she encountered. If her sisters or my father didn't fix things, then she would look to us kids to step in. The healthy coping skills she needed to live in an adult world were greatly compromised. She developed powerfully maladaptive ones in order to decrease her mounting anxieties. My mother was not motivated to grow and develop intellectually or emotionally. Mama seemed to have no internal apparatus for control, no way to regulate her overwhelming anxieties and fears, and certainly no way to make good decisions.

Chapter 2

She Found Stable Ground

My second view of motherhood as a child came by watching my father's mother. Maw Maw Linnie personified the American ideal of motherhood. She was a faithful, loving, generous spirit. Her love for her entire family was sacrificial and welcoming.

My paternal grandparents, Evelyn "Linnie" and Frazier Gryce O'Neal, named my father Herman Troy. My father called himself Patrick O'Neal because when he was a youngster, his beloved Uncle Harmon Rayner (after whom his parents named him) had fondly called him "Paddy" and the name stuck. From then on, he was known as Patrick Herman O'Neal. Daddy was the youngest living child of the six children born to my grandparents.

One younger son, Brewster Bernard "Scrap," died after contracting polio at the age of five, on July 10, 1929. Daddy said he was a virtual genius. The school system had tested him and would have promoted him several grades had he not passed away. All of the surviving children—four sons (Frazier "Wig," Ray, Darlie D., and my father) and one daughter (Mabel)—were devoted to their mother.

Everyone in Ball, Louisiana, knew Linnie O'Neal. She was of solid Scotch Irish stock. Her father, Andrew Jackson Rayner, married Lydia Candace Finney on her twentieth birthday, February 18, 1882, in Washington County, Mississippi. Lydia's family, the W. W. Finneys, strongly objected to the union because the two were first cousins. Their mothers were sisters. A family feud ensued once the couple eloped.

The Finneys moved to Chicot County, Arkansas. They eventually forgave the young couple and invited them to come to Arkansas to live. Andrew and Lydia lived there from the fall of 1882 until 1897 when Andrew moved his large family to Ball, a small sawmill community in north Rapides Parish, Louisiana.

In Ball, he purchased a large tract of timberland. Once settled, he began cutting and selling pine logs to the nearby sawmill. Ander, as the family knew him, removed the timber and then farmed the land and raised cattle and hogs. Family members remembered him as a hard worker who annually covered a hilltop on his property with strawberries or melons he propagated in the house prior to planting.

Great-Grandpa Andrew lost his beloved Lydia on April 28, 1918, after a lengthy illness. My father told me that his grandfather mourned for her until the day he died, never having remarried. Andrew died on September 19, 1929. He was buried in the peacefully quaint Springhill Cemetery next to Lydia in a section designated for the Rayner and O'Neal families. (Springhill Cemetery lies northwest of Ball; it's located in the Simms community right across the Rapides Parish line in Grant Parish.)

Maw Maw Linnie was born on September 29, 1886, in Chicot County, Arkansas, as the second oldest of the seven children of Andrew and Lydia. She was only eleven when her parents moved to Ball. Many folks in the community called her "Aunt Linnie," whether they were related to her or not. She was much loved and considered akin to a saint. Her children adored her, especially my father.

My grandmother Linnie experienced the loss of her young husband, Frazier O'Neal, on July 23, 1924, when baby Scrap was only four months old. Left to rear six children alone, she endured the Great Depression of the 1930s as a single mother. Her life's situation tempered her to become tenacious and cautious, especially about spending beyond her means. She had to be extra thrifty during those trying years. Maw Maw Linnie knew how to stretch a dollar and could take a small amount of food and feed an army.

My paternal grandfather, Frazier, had been a rounder of sorts who liked to drink and flirt with the women. He was a small-framed Irishman who was good looking, wiry, and apparently not fearful of taking on any perceived threat. This wild-boy attitude became a detrimental characteristic in that his lack of fear led to his early demise.

A horse Grandpa Frazier owned was stolen from him by a man named Buford Cole. My grandfather heard that Cole had sold the horse to a local merchant named McArthur. He went by horseback to confront McArthur at his mercantile located roughly six miles south of Ball in an area called Kingsville.

This was the midpoint between the city of Pineville in central Rapides Parish and Ball at the northernmost part of Rapides. Daddy said that in his youth they called it the "end of the flat pavement" because from there, north to Ball, was nothing but a gravel road frequented by horses or horse-drawn wagons.

Sitting astride his horse, Grandpa Frazier called the merchant out. McArthur emerged with a loaded shotgun. He stood on the high delivery porch of his establishment as Grandpa Frazier questioned him. An argument ensued, which then became heated. McArthur made a motion that spooked Grandpa Frazier's horse. The horse reared up and then spun around. As the horse turned, it put my grandfather level with the merchant. McArthur stuck his shotgun in my grandfather's side and pulled the trigger.

The horse continued the long journey back to Ball with its mane smoldering as Grandpa Frazier slumped low over its neck. The loyal animal delivered Grandpa to the porch of his own home where Maw Maw Linnie received the mortally wounded father of her children. My grandfather lingered for a day before dying. His body was laid out for viewing on the dining-room table prior to burial.

Local law enforcement arrested McArthur for his crime, and he went to trial. Family lore says that he and Buford Cole paid a few people to testify that they witnessed Grandpa Frazier pulling a pistol on McArthur. For that reason, McArthur was acquitted and released. Several male family members wanted to kill Buford Cole for his part in the dirty dealings. I suppose they thought better of it since Maw Maw Linnie was going to need all the help she could get. Justice came in part when McArthur subsequently lost his sanity. Some family members felt that his guilt eventually drove him over the edge.

Maw Maw Linnie's brothers George, Harmon, and Leroy Rayner were loving and loyal toward her. They had been the support and assistance she needed in order to rear her orphaned children. The O'Neals and Rayners raised much of the food they needed and shared among themselves. The uncles taught the boys how to hunt, fish, tend to cattle, and raise a garden so they would never go hungry.

The community saying was that Linnie O'Neal never met a stranger. Although she didn't venture far from her home, whoever came to her door was welcomed and fed physically and spiritually. She never turned anyone in need away.

During World War II, there was a large army camp on the eastern edge of Ball called Camp Livingston. The camp facilitated quite an economic boon to this area. Livingston was large enough to attract the attention of celebrities who came to entertain the troops. Once, the famous Gypsy Rose Lee came there to do her patriotic part!

Soldiers from all over the United States were stationed there. Often their girlfriends or wives would travel by bus to come to Louisiana to visit their soldier boys. The Greyhound bus stopped on US 165 directly in front of Maw Maw Linnie's white frame home.

There was very little to offer in the way of places to stay or restaurants and cafes. My grandmother would take the bewildered and frightened women in and offer them a place to rest and a bite to eat before resuming their journey. It was unheard of for someone to take in an African American or Hispanic person in those days in our part of the world, but she did. Moreover, nobody called her on it! They didn't dare! Everyone was a child of God in Linnie O'Neal's eyes. I'm sure my grandmother sensed the wounded child who was my mother and embraced her into the family as one of her own for that very reason.

My grandmother lived on the corner of US 165 North (also known as the Monroe Highway) and the Ball Cut-Off Road. Ball was a small, rural community in the 1960s, but is now a thriving little town of Rapides Parish. Geographically, it is the center of the state of Louisiana, a crossroad between the widely disparate cultures of the northern and southern portions of the state. Ball is located on the periphery of the Kisatchie National Forest. The area had plentiful, towering virgin pine trees, with lush spring and summer vegetation in the vast pastures of my youth.

Central Louisiana and north to Shreveport is predominantly the Bible Belt of the state. My sisters, brother, and I were not exposed to the spicy culture of south Louisiana until we were adults. Our community religious base in Ball was Southern Baptist and Pentecostal—folks considered Roman Catholics to be worshipers of statues of Jesus and Mary, and Jews to be tight with their money.

As a child of the '60s, I deplored the prejudices and racism I encountered not only in the community, but also from some of my own family members. Daddy and Maw Maw Linnie never treated people in that judgmental way. They were the models my siblings and I most patterned our belief systems after. I don't ever remember my grandmother Linnie attending church; however, she read the Bible and was a godly, spiritual woman. She lived the tenets of a Christian life.

Daddy didn't embrace organized religion because he said he had seen too much hypocrisy among so-called Christians. He was, however, one of the most spiritual people I ever knew. He studied the Bible and knew its contents better than most churchgoing folks did. Daddy believed that some higher power much greater than man could ever fathom had created our world and us. His beliefs were based on the faith and perseverance he saw in his mother and uncles.

Daddy was also a lifelong student of nature and the cycles of life and death he witnessed in the Louisiana woodlands. Near the end of his life, he said that if he could have afforded a nice camera with a telescopic lens he would have liked to photograph the woods he knew. Instead of taking home a trophy buck or a fat black squirrel, he began to believe that the real prize would have been to show everyone how that deer or squirrel looked in its natural environment.

Several of Daddy's siblings lived away from Ball. His older brothers, Ray (who worked for a natural gas company) and Darlie D. (who was in the Air Force), lived elsewhere with their wives and children. We would see their families periodically when they came to visit Maw Maw Linnie.

The O'Neal boys' only sister, Mabel, had never been too happy in provincial Ball. She also hated the name Grandpa Frazier gave her, supposedly after one of his "women friends." She unofficially changed her name to Kitty, although her brothers never quit calling her Mabel.

Aunt Kitty was my hero when I was a child. Sometimes she would come to stay or visit Maw Maw Linnie while her husband, Denny, a career military man, was stationed out of the United States. I looked forward to her stays because she brought a piece of the outside world to Ball.

I have a vivid memory of walking down Maw Maw Linnie's long driveway lined with stately virgin pines to meet Aunt Kitty when she came home on a Greyhound bus. I could always count on her bringing me some little present. One particular time it was a long, twisted, black stick of candy. This was something I had never seen. I took a big bite of it and thought it tasted awful! What in the world had she given me? I'm sure she must have seen the look on my face because she quickly tried to explain to me what licorice was. She told me that she thought I might want to try something new.

All I thought was how to be polite, how to finish the chewy wad, and how not to show my ignorance by spitting it on the dusty driveway. I thought this was something fancy people gave to their children. I hoped she never brought me another piece!

Aunt Kitty was vibrant, alive, and creative. Her daughters, Denette and Denise, were charged with that same electric spirit. When they came home to Ball, they brought excitement into my world. I hung on their every word. I could hear refinement in their manner of speaking. They knew things about the world that were foreign to me, but that I wished and hoped to know. As a kid, I thought about how Aunt Kitty had made it out of our hick community and if she could do it, so could I!

Daddy was proud of his sister. He talked about how she could take something that had little value to others and then turn it into something beautiful. Once, he told me how she had written a letter home to Maw Maw Linnie requesting burlap croker sacks. My sweet grandmother couldn't imagine why Mabel wanted those old feed sacks, especially since she was living on a military base where she could have purchased anything she needed. However, Aunt Kitty had seen her mother take those same cast-off burlap and/or cotton sacks and make something useable out of them. Maw Maw Linnie made several A-line "princess" dresses for me using printed, cotton feed sacks.

Daddy said Aunt Kitty wanted to make her house look as good as the homes of the commissioned officers' wives. She couldn't afford expensive drapes. Instead, she took the burlap sacks Maw Maw Linnie sent her, ripped the seams, dyed them a fashionable ochre color, and sewed them into drapes. All the women on the base were envious of her new acquisition—they just didn't know she hadn't paid a fortune for them.

Aunt Kitty was considerate of Mama in a compassionate way. I could always sense that she pitied Mama as being unschooled and ignorant, but she didn't hold that against her. I recall that she tried to help Mama by guiding her in the adult world. I think Mama respected her on some level, but there was resentment there too. Aunt Kitty knew how the world outside of Ball operated; she could negotiate it. She knew what she wanted out of life and wasn't shy about expressing it. I believe Mama saw that as threatening and foreign to her way of thinking. Aunt Kitty was not the sort of woman Mama could connect with about life.

Daddy's brother Wig never ventured too far away from central Louisiana. He was an important character in much of my childhood. As a toddler, I can remember him being at Maw Maw Linnie's frequently and then living there after he divorced. When I smell wood smoke, I think of him. Maw Maw Linnie used a wood-burning, pot-bellied stove for heat and some cooking in the winter months. Uncle Wig usually tended to this chore so that he could keep his Mama supplied with kindling and chopped wood. The earthy smell of the outdoors and wood smoke clung to his body like a second skin. He almost seemed out of place indoors.

Janis and I went to Maw Maw Linnie's every day. Uncle Wig was usually in the backyard tending to a garden or the chickens. Sometimes we could see him squatting next to the porch as we approached the house. Uncle Wig was the only adult I knew who was more comfortable squatting close to the ground like a little leprechaun than he was sitting in a chair in the house. His delicate wire-framed glasses perched high on the bridge of his nose seemed incongruous against his weather-darkened skin.

He'd ask, "What you Injuns up to today?" as he deftly shook his Bugler tobacco into the thin white paper he held between his nicotine-darkened thumb and forefinger. We would stop and stare as he licked the edge of the transparent paper and then roll it into a bumpy cylinder before placing it into the corner of his mouth. He usually had to blow stray pieces of tobacco off his lip before he struck the match on the thigh of his khakis. With cupped hands around the flame and eyes squeezed against the smoke he'd ask, "Where's your daddy?"

Uncle Wig was a small and leathery man, but he knew the woods and streams around us better than anyone I knew. He was sometimes ornery and he was a drunk, but he loved us kids and looked out for us for the most part. He and my mother despised each other at times and at other times they got along. They had a mutual need to use each other over the years, and, to borrow a line from Bob Seger, "neither one cared!" Daddy had to referee their squabbles continually—Mama didn't like it if Daddy sided with Uncle Wig.

Uncle Wig's first wife, Opal, and he divorced when their two children were very young. Near the end of his life, he married again, a woman named Goldie. They were living in Grant Parish near Little River when he died. He was a man who would have fared well in the rough and rugged days of the Old West. Uncle Wig reminded me of the Hank Williams, Jr. song, "A Country Boy Can Survive," running trotlines and skinning squirrels and deer. Daddy often said that people like him would survive if the apocalypse came; they could take care of themselves out on Little River or Hard Water Lake. Being around civilized people was much more frightening to Uncle Wig than coming face to face with a timber rattler.

Daddy's extended family was as important to him as his siblings were. Maw Maw Linnie was a Rayner by birth. She and her brother Leroy married O'Neal siblings: Frazier and Maude. The offspring these two couples produced were known as double first cousins. Much was made of this connection, and the cousins considered themselves as close as siblings. Great Uncle Leroy and Aunt Maude sired four sons and one daughter. Both families shared adjoining property with home sites nearby. They were proud of their Irish heritage and were clannish in their sensibilities.

Daddy was especially fond of his younger cousin Loren Dale, who everybody called "Frog." Frog was a strapping, good-looking young man. He and his sister, Shirley, favored each other. Both had lean, chiseled features, black hair, and dark eyes. They liked to say that they were Black Irish and had Native American blood. Daddy didn't agree with the Indian notion, but he did say they represented the Black Irish side of the family and his side represented the Red Irish.

Frog and Daddy "ran" together, worked together, and, after Frog returned from active duty in the navy during the Korean Conflict, they built homes on their pieces of O'Neal and Rayner property near each other. The O'Neal and Rayner families were accepting and inclusive of my mother.

Frog's wife, Marjory "Marbeth," was probably the female closest to being my mother's one true friend. She was a lively, fair-skinned, freckle-faced doe of a girl, long and lean. Marbeth never met a stranger; she was welcoming and generous.

My mother and Marbeth were very young, newlywed women who had come from poor backgrounds and in close order brought several children into the world during the mid to late '50s. They bonded rather quickly, which was a good thing. I'm inclined to think that if Marbeth had not been so nearby, some of Mama's anger may not have had an outlet for expression. She possibly could have done serious physical harm to us children had there not been a sympathetic ear available so that she could air her frustrations. I know Marbeth was instrumental in providing my brother, Oscar, a safe haven away from Mama's tirades as the years passed.

Marbeth and Frog had four children, two girls and two boys, close in age to my siblings and me. Of those four, the oldest boy, Jimmy Dale, or Pogo, as he was known, was as close to Oscar as our daddy was to his daddy. Daddy and Frog took those two boys hunting and fishing from the time they were old enough to hold a fishing pole. It was nothing for Oscar and Pogo to go off to the creek to fish for bream or sun perch or to swim for hours at a time when they were only eight or nine years old. Marbeth would stand on her back porch, bright sunlight reflecting off her strawberry blond hair, calling the boys to come in to eat.

Shirley Jean, the youngest child of their family, was also an important character in my family's early years. She was only a bit younger than Mama and Marbeth. Shirley never married, so she spent much of her time with the two of them. Shirley was a little eccentric. She dressed like a man and kept her blue-black hair cut short. I fondly remember the rolled-up blue jeans and brown penny loafers she wore (with a real penny in each one). Although she was an odd duck who caused the neighborhood tongues to wag, she had one of the kindest, most loving hearts I have ever known.

Shirley was attentive toward me. She used to brush my long, dishwater blond hair and tell me stories. Once, she taught me how to create a makeshift toothbrush by using a stem from a sweet gum tree. She showed me how to peel the bark back about half an inch, exposing the greenish-white inner wood. Then we used a paring knife to make tiny crisscrossed cuts that made the green wood began to bristle into tiny strands. Shirley said that's what she used when she went camping with Uncle Leroy and her brothers and didn't have a toothbrush. She told me to pour a little salt in my hand, wet the sweet gum brush, stick it in the salt and then into my mouth, and scrub away. She said, "There you go—clean teeth!"

We didn't attend church as a family; what little I knew about religion, before going to school, was what Daddy told me about Jesus and about what he had read in the Bible. Daddy's words made me picture Jesus as a loving, kind spirit who loved little children.

Shirley gave me my first dose of Christian religious reality. On a beautiful, deep sapphire evening as I watched millions of stars twinkle in the heavens out in our front yard, she told me how God would cause the world to come to a fiery end. I stood on a wooden picnic table under the sweet gum tree and listened to her talk. The more she talked, the more frightened I became.

Lip trembling, I asked, "Why would God do that?"

"Because people are bad, they sin—but at least he won't bring a flood to cover the world like he did the first time," Shirley told me.

I didn't understand, and I didn't want to understand—I ran into the house crying. Daddy chastised Shirley, "Why in the world would you tell her that, Shirley?" She was mortified that she had upset me; she hadn't meant any harm.

Shirley and Daddy shared a common, innate compassion that permeated every fiber of their beings. It was as if they possessed an extra sense that kept them acutely in tune with another being's pain. They were incredibly tenderhearted and couldn't bear the suffering they witnessed in other people or animals. Daddy was fond of Shirley. He worried about her all her life because she didn't fit everyone's idea of the norm.

Mama also had an extra sensibility—a gift for recognizing vulnerability in those who peopled her existence. Shirley was one of those people. She loved Mama and affectionately called her "Cuz."

When Mama got on one of her griping or gossipy tirades, Shirley would good-naturedly say, "Aw, Cuz, that ain't any way to be."

Mama's standard reply was, "Shut up, Shirley Jean Rayner, you don't know what the hell you're talking about!"

Mama could manipulate her quite well. She used Shirley as an advocate and a mouthpiece in order to shore up her need for dominance in the family setting. Shirley would champion Mama because she felt sorry for her. Marbeth stood her ground with Mama. Although she was empathetic, and because she believed Mama didn't know better, she never let her get away with the complete monopolization of the relationship as Mama so often did with Shirley.

The O'Neals and Rayners accepted Mama into their midst with open arms. She became as much a part of the extended family as if she had been born to it. In many ways, I think my mother believed this was her true family. She sometimes exhibited a loyalty to the family that was hard to define. Mama never overtly expressed a genuine statement to any of us about how she felt about us. However, sometimes an odd sort of pride would develop in her voice when she talked about the O'Neal family to outsiders. I know, without a doubt, that Marbeth, Shirley, and Maw Maw Linnie were stabilizing influences for Mama in the early years. In Ball, Mama found stability and permanence that she had not known with her own family.

Chapter 3

The Early Years on Ball Cut-Off Road

I firmly believe that my father married my mother to rescue her. At the tender age of sixteen, she was petite and quite voluptuous, with a full head of wavy brunette hair. Although functionally illiterate, something willfully intelligent and powerfully mesmerizing emerged from her hazel-green eyes in the few pictures I have seen of her at that time.

My father's boyish good looks, easy grin, and wavy brown hair belied the fact that he was ten years Mama's senior. He was back from serving in World War II and was somewhat of a wild, Irish bantam rooster. Apparently, Maw Maw Lavinia had no qualms about her youngest daughter being courted by an older man. After all, she had a pattern of marrying older men herself. I imagine that Maw Maw Lavinia estimated that Christine had gotten herself quite a catch. She gave Daddy no resistance, which inclines me to believe that she was relieved to let her young daughter go.

I have no doubt Daddy was looking for a mate, someone to bear his children. There was probably a strong, immediate sexual bond between him and my mother. I knew my father's heart well; I believe he intended to nurture and care for this woman-child in a way that her family wouldn't or couldn't. They married on April 28, 1951.

Mama trusted Daddy. In her way of thinking, Daddy was the final word for the way things should be. She counted on his knowledge of the world. She looked to him to show her how things needed to be done. He was educated, had traveled somewhat, and knew about things she could never hope to, or for that matter to even want to know. She was dependent on him. When it came to conducting the business of living, he was her authority.

She did challenge him about many issues during their years together; petty, nonsensical issues that would lead to arguments and fights. However, he was the anchor for her existence. Whatever Pat said or "your daddy" declared, in her mind, was the gospel. I believe she saw him as a parental figure. He was good to her, patient with her, and tolerant, sometimes to everyone's detriment. She would use this basic goodness against him as her anxieties and manipulative nature grew.

I was born on January 31, 1953. My father was working the pipeline in the small town of Smithville, Texas. Daddy had started working the Texas oil pipeline soon after he and Mama married. They had to leave Ball, but according to Daddy, the money was too good to pass up.

Apparently, Mama was in labor quite some time. Daddy rode out the night in the waiting room of the town's small clinic. He told the story of that night often. That January night, he said, was very cold, with loud, violent gusts of blowing rain. The winter storm added to his nervous state as he sat awaiting my birth.

At one point, he said, the doors swung open like in a movie, and a young, very pregnant Mexican girl came through the doors alone. Attendants rushed her through to labor and delivery. About five minutes later, my father heard a newborn's cry. He excitedly ran to the doors. The staff told him that the crying baby was not his. Amazingly, fifteen minutes later, the Mexican girl walked out of delivery with the swaddled baby and disappeared into the night. I have wondered what path lay ahead for the two of them.

I can imagine my mother being terrified and feeling alone, away from home, in the midst of strangers, delivering a child she was ill equipped to care for at the age of eighteen. Apparently, it was a difficult birth. I was born with my left hand bent forward toward my wrist. My left ear was folded over toward my face, leaving it very bruised. My father told me the physicians thought I was "Mongoloid"; that was the term used then for Down syndrome children. They also informed him that I would need surgery to correct the wrist and ear. Daddy was stunned by this news.

Mama told me she tried to nurse me "on the breast," which I'm sure my father had encouraged her to do as the natural way to feed a child. Apparently, her milk didn't come down soon enough and I was starving. Daddy went to the doctor to see what I could be given. Mama shared with me many years later that the doctor recommended canned milk, which Daddy went out to find for me. She also told me that they had no crib for me. Daddy transformed a dresser drawer into a bed for me. As I grew up, it was Daddy who talked to me about my infancy and the events surrounding my birth and our subsequent move back to Ball, Louisiana.

Shortly after my birth, Daddy got a letter from Shirley, telling him that Maw Maw Linnie was sick with blood poisoning. Shirley told him that his mother had been admitted to Murrells's Clinic in Alexandria for treatment. As soon as he got the letter he told Mama to pack up, they were going home to take care of his mama. I think he was also concerned about Mama's ability to care for a potentially handicapped child. Daddy may have been prompted to leave Texas and a good-paying job to go back home not only to take care of his mother, but also so that my mother could receive Linnie's guidance.

Daddy moved us back to Ball where we lived for a time in Maw Maw Linnie's house. My grandmother took me into her big, old feather bed and cared for me. She and my father were the nurturers, the comforters. Daddy worked with my wrist and ear by manipulating the bruised tissue using his fingers and lips to massage the tender flesh. Gradually, the blood flow to my ear and hand normalized because of his tender, therapeutic, care—no surgery was required!

My grandmother welcomed my mother in and treated her as one of her own. Mama came with limited domestic skills, but Maw Maw Linnie patiently worked with Mama until she could manage the most basic cooking and laundry duties. I don't believe anybody had ever taken the time to teach my mother anything or to treat her in any fashion as an adult. My grandmother's patient nature was such that she lovingly reached out to those in need and provided them with whatever she had to offer, no questions asked. Maw Maw Linnie lived humbly and quietly. Given time, my mother was able to adopt a semblance of a style of life she had not been accustomed to before.

Maw Maw Linnie had been given a sizeable piece of property by her brothers. The property extended about an acre and a half along US 165 and about four or five acres along Ball Cut-Off Road. During my childhood, none of her children lived on the property. Once Daddy returned to Louisiana with his young family, he felt a strong sense of obligation to look after us as well as his beloved mama. She gave him roughly two acres of land fronted by the Ball Cut-Off Road. He had to clear it of dense underbrush and sapling pines in order to establish a home site for us.

There he built our first home, a shotgun-style frame house. That description derived from the notion that if you were to fire a shotgun through the front door of such a house, the bullet would make a straight path through the house and emerge out the back door. It had a combination kitchen-living room and a bedroom. I don't know if it had a bathroom or not. I vaguely remember the house because we rode out Hurricane Audrey in it.

That historic hurricane hit Cameron Parish in the southern portion of Louisiana in late June 1957. I can recall the anxiety and fear my parents felt about our safety as the wind howled and the rain pinged steadily in buckets Daddy had set around the tiny house. We were hundreds of miles away from landfall, but she still kicked our butt.

Even though I was only four years old, I can remember walking around my grandmother's enormous yard with Daddy the next day. We surveyed the damage from the torrential rain and wind. There were huge, downed limbs from the old pine trees and millions of green pinecones that appeared to have rained down from the sky, scattered everywhere over that acreage. The smell of pine resin wafted through the air as Daddy and I walked over a carpet of bright, green needles that made our walk-about seem eerily quiet.

I don't recall my mother ever talking in depth about her pregnancies. She also didn't talk about how she felt about motherhood. I do recall her saying things, however, about how pregnancy affected her, with all her aches and pains. She did not seem to derive any joy from the experiences.

Some family members have told me that Mama loved us as babies. That seemed to me to be a strange thing for them to say. It was as if we were like kittens or baby bunnies—warm and cuddly, soft and easy to love until we started to grow and became real work for her. Babies can't tell anyone if they've been pinched or beaten. I believe my siblings and I weren't a threat to her as long as we were incapable of verbally communicating with our father. Maw Maw Linnie's art of mothering is what I remember more than any motherly display from Mama.

Maw Maw Linnie's strength and perseverance were held in high esteem by all who knew her. She was the wellspring, the source of comfort and stability we all sought. I never recall my mother being affectionate toward my sister Janis and me. Janis arrived eighteen months after my birth. I do remember my paternal grandmother's loving, easy touch and her soothing ways. Maw Maw Linnie adored us, probably much to the chagrin of our other cousins who didn't live in such close proximity. She fondly called Janis Marie her "Jannie-Re," which I shortened to Ye.

Janis was born in Alexandria on September 8, 1954. We had a special sisterly bond. She was like my little baby doll—a squat, round treasure. Her blond cap of tight curls accentuated her wide-open, happy face. I looked after her and packed her on my hip everywhere we went. Maw Maw Linnie would scold me and say I needed to quit packing that big "young'un" because I was going to end up with kidney problems. I didn't care; I was her protector, and I needed to take care of her.

We made our visits to see Maw Maw Linnie almost every day. Janis and I went so often, we created a well-worn trail to her house through what we thought of as vast woods. Pine trees, pin oaks, a mulberry tree, poison ivy, briars, and barbed wire lined that trail. Nothing, not the woods, ticks, cockleburs, or even the dreaded snakes in our path could keep us from Maw

Maw. If we did encounter a snake, for a while we would avoid the woods and go by way of the blacktopped Ball Cut-Off Road—we liked to pop tar bubbles with our bare toes.

We were free to be, under Maw Maw Linnie's watchful eye. The conviction that she was our daily protector probably helped save Janis and me one time when we were about seven and eight. Early one afternoon, we took the slightly longer road route. We were just about to cross over a steep ditch to access the far corner of Maw Maw Linnie's yard when a car slowed down next to Janis. I had already made the jump but turned to say something to my sister. There were two men in the large, four-door car. A young black man was driving and an older, white man was seated on the passenger side. His door was open. Janis was silhouetted by the frame of the big car door.

The man was still seated but had swung his legs out onto the road—I could see his oversized, brown, lace-up shoes pointed in my direction. I watched as the man leaned forward, placing his left hand on Janis's shoulder.

I don't remember crossing back over the ditch; I just remember reaching my sister's side. The man gestured with his right hand. "We're trying to find . . ." I couldn't understand the rest of the statement. I was concentrating on how odd it seemed that he had on a long-sleeved dress shirt on such a warm day. *Was he a businessman?* I thought. Something didn't feel right.

Nervously, I told him that we had to get to our grandmother's house. I put my hand around Janis's wrist saying, "Come on, we gotta go."

As I tugged, I could feel the pressure of the man's hand on Janis's shoulder, keeping her from moving. He said for us to get in the car, that they could give us a ride. Janis began crying; I began babbling and crying. I told the man that we didn't need a ride, that we didn't know the place he was looking for but that our grandmother could tell him.

"See, she lives right there," I said, pointing at her house. "She's waiting for us on her back porch; we have to go."

I began a desperate struggle to release my sister from the man's grip. The more he insisted that we get in the car, the louder Janis and I bawled. I remember that the men exchanged looks—I couldn't read their faces; I was too scared. Just as suddenly as the episode began, it ended. The man took his hand off Janis's arm. Both of us ran as if a mad blue-runner snake was after us.

Breathlessly, we reached Maw Maw Linnie's porch steps and then pounded across the wood expanse. Maw Maw Linnie met us at the screen door. Excitedly, we told her about the men. A deep look of concern crossed her face, but she never showed panic. She told us that from then on she wanted us to come to her house by way of our trail. As she turned to go into the house, she said we never could be sure about what mischief men might be up to out there.

Maw Maw Linnie allowed us to explore the surrounding grounds of her rural domain, liberally testing the boundaries of country life. I remember when we robbed her heavily guarded hen house, narrowly missing the vicious spurs of her blue-black rooster, Smokey Joe. We took those stolen eggs and made the best mud pie Ball had ever seen! Other than a slight scolding, we were allowed an opportunity to play creatively. Mama chastised her mother-in-law for letting us get away with murder, but Maw Maw Linnie just shook her head and said. "Now Christine, they're only babies once, and it's awright."

Daddy knew Maw Maw Linnie's health was failing, so he watched protectively over her, indulging her little whims and eccentricities. My grandmother had never learned to drive and so someone had to "carry" her to town to purchase groceries or other needed items.

Daddy would laugh and say, "Mama always wants to save a few pennies by cutting out all the coupons from the local newspaper, the *Alexandria Daily Town Talk*. Poor thing, she doesn't realize it takes a full tank of gas to take her to all those places to buy her sale items." However, it didn't matter—if his Mama needed to go to the far reaches of the state, Daddy would have done it for her. Moreover, the rest of the family would have too.

I think Mama loved and respected Maw Maw Linnie as much as she was capable of loving and respecting another human. Through the years, she would refer to her as "that old woman," but it wasn't necessarily said in a malicious tone. I believe my grandmother showed Mama genuine regard and treated her as capable, as someone with potential. Under Maw Maw Linnie's tutelage, Mama learned how to cook and to take care of a home.

The memories I have retained of those years are mostly pleasant. Maw Maw Linnie became our source of refuge, comfort, and security. She wasn't an externally beautiful woman. Maw Maw Linnie might have been considered a bit plain with her slightly bulbous Irish nose, high cheekbones, and wide brow set on a round face. Nevertheless, she had impishly twinkling blue-green eyes and a wonderfully sweet voice, a welcoming smile and disposition. She could wrap us to her matronly bosom and make all our sorrows go away.

Janis and I spent hours of play when we were toddlers at Maw Maw Linnie's home in a poor, albeit idyllic setting. We were wild and free country girls running around barefoot with nothing on except our "step-ins" (panties). I loved to sit on her front porch where I would get that sleepy déjà vu feeling of having always been right there smelling the musty sweet smell of ligustrum and honeysuckle or picking the hard, black seeds from the center of the colorful four-o'clocks growing wildly by the steps.

Her yard was vast, and those towering pine trees stood sentry along each side of the dirt driveway leading to her white, frame home. The driveway seemed to be miles long when I was a child. It felt comforting to walk along it in the early spring when the snowbells and narcissus Maw Maw Linnie had planted bloomed in straight paths along the driveway. We picked handfuls and sniffed their delicate fragrance as we took them back to Maw Maw to place in a Kerr jar on her windowsill.

Our territory for play was mainly around the house perimeter; it wasn't safe to stray too far into the yard. Daddy and Maw Maw Linnie constantly warned of snakes around the pines, especially the deadly, shy coral snakes and the nasty-tempered ground rattlers and copperhead snakes. Janis and I dug in the rich dirt in Maw Maw Linnie's backyard under the sassafras and fig trees. When the Louisiana spring quickly became summer, we walked barefoot on the driveway in the shadows of the pine trees, protected from sharp rocks or sticks by the comforting softness of the degrading, rust-colored pine straw.

In the spring and summer, Maw Maw Linnie made lemonade for us in a blue crockery pitcher. She called us in each noon to eat smothered okra or cabbage, cornbread, fresh sliced tomatoes, and slow-simmered chicken she stewed down in a black iron skillet. The smell of summer would fill the kitchen when she cut up fresh cucumbers in a bowl of vinegar liberally sprinkled with black pepper.

We went with her to search the barbed-wire fencerows for elusive, lush blackberries or dewberries, carefully avoiding the thorns and snakes as we reached into the deep foliage hiding those luscious treats. We brought the berries back to her house, and after she carefully washed them, she would make us wonderful delicacies like blackberry cobbler.

At the height of summer, various people in the neighborhood habitually brought Maw Maw Linnie fresh vegetables: bushel baskets of purple-hull peas, tomatoes, peaches, pears, or new potatoes. Janis and I learned how to help her pull the green husks off the corn and then strip it of its dark, pungent silk. After cleaning the corn, she scraped the kernels off and then smothered them down in a skillet. We sat on her back porch and shelled butter beans and other kinds of peas until our fingertips were sore and wrinkled.

Maw Maw Linnie canned or preserved much of the produce she was given. I loved the days when she got just-picked fruit, like peaches. She told us we had to eat them out in the yard because once we took a big bite, juice would run down our chins and arms. I wasn't fond of helping pick figs—the big, hairy leaves were hard to avoid and made my skin itch. The result of that prickly chore was luscious, plump, sweet fig preserves.

When fall arrived, she used the preserved fruit to make cobblers or pies. Maw Maw Linnie liked to tease us when she made raisin pies. She said they were "tick pies." I think it tickled her to hear us squeal at the absurdity of such a thing. Sometimes her offering might be "poor man's" (bread) pudding or rice pudding she made using leftover day-old bread or rice.

She was only slightly indulgent, with a round, warm, sweet-tempered place to land when we needed comforting. She doted on Janis and me. She told us we were her special babies. I remember burying my head in her lap many times. At those times, she softly spoke to me, rubbed my hair, and gave me solace when someone hurt my feelings. She allowed me to stand on a stool behind her rocking chair to comb and brush her wavy, dark hair, never complaining, even though I almost "pulled her bald," as Daddy would later say.

Relatives and neighbors loved to visit Aunt Linnie, not only for her cooking, but because they loved her hospitality. They especially loved her fresh-brewed coffee with real cream or biscuits dripping with butter. Janis and I "helped" her churn that butter in an old crockery churn.

Maw Maw Linnie had a well house, close to her wooden chicken house, where we accompanied her to retrieve ice-cold water that I never liked because it had a metallic taste. Another chore she allowed us to participate in was feeding the chickens and collecting the eggs in an old, worn basket.

I was fascinated by the glass eggs she kept in the hen house. "What are these for, Maw Maw?" I asked.

She explained that chicken snakes, which might grow to be six or seven feet long, often slithered through the cracks in the chicken coop in order to feed on unattended eggs or newly hatched chicks. When they slithered back out the crack, the fragile chicken eggs that they had swallowed completely were crushed, allowing the snake to return to the bushes to digest the stolen sustenance. The snake didn't know the difference between an actual egg and the glass egg. Once it swallowed a fake egg, the snake became trapped because the heavy glass egg wasn't as easily broken as the chicken egg. Maw Maw Linnie said she was able to chop the head off those thieving boogers when she found them stuck like that.

When I was a first grader, as part of the Easter festivities at Paradise Elementary, the students were offered an opportunity to enter an Easter bonnet contest. Maw Maw Linnie and Aunt Kitty, who was visiting at the time, made a bonnet for me. They took a large Chore Girl pot scrubber and pulled and stretched the copper wire until it resembled a bird's nest. Aunt Kitty stuck pine straw, downy chicken breast feathers, and small twigs in between the wire to make it more realistic looking; then Maw Maw Linnie placed some tiny blown-out "banty" (bantam) eggs inside. After attaching satin ribbon to the sides, they placed it on my head and tied the ribbon under my chin. The lopsided little nest tilted alarmingly, but I managed to keep it balanced and wore it to school. I won an honorable mention.

I associate eggs, so symbolic of the richness of the life cycle, with the grandmother who so dearly loved me.

I suppose Janis and I were very fortunate that Maw Maw Linnie was watching over us as much as she did. I don't believe Mama could have handled the pressure of our care if she had been completely alone. As an adult, Frog shared a family secret with me, which became another unraveling of the knot surrounding my mother's behavior.

Frog indicated to me that Daddy had told him the story several times. He related how when I was about a year and a half, maybe two years old, Daddy came home from work one day to find Mama beating me down on the floor with her fists. They had to take me to the hospital. Mama swore that I had fallen from my high chair and that's why I had two black eyes.

I always wondered why in my elementary school pictures I had a noticeable, reddish mark under my right eye. It was painful to hear that story because I didn't have any indication that Mama had been physically abusive toward me as an infant. I have vivid memories of her abusive hand in later years. That story might also explain the strange statement family members used when they tried to convince my siblings and me that Mama had loved us as babies. I could never reconcile that sentiment because I never felt that she loved me at any time.

As I record this, it seems very odd to me that I can't remember much of my mother during my toddler years. The exception is the scrubbing episode in the galvanized tub when Mama attacked my flesh with the washcloth as if she meant to scrub away my very soul. The tub was out back behind Maw Maw Linnie's house. I remember my mother's sister Claudie standing there with her.

I can still see the deep green, wide-leafed fig trees and hear the sound of my grandmother's chickens as Mama scrubbed me in that tub. I remember feeling embarrassed and ashamed under a darkening sky. The reason for the scrubbing was because my aunt's two older boys, Junior and Ray, who couldn't have been much older than me, had caught up with me behind Maw Maw Linnie's chicken coop and persuaded me to pull down my panties. The two women came upon that scene, and all hell broke loose.

I have never wanted to tell anyone about the incident. It made me feel dirty to think about it. I had no love for those boy cousins, but not because I thought they had harmed me. In all honesty, I think it was childhood curiosity, but I suppose Mama was convinced that they had molested me.

I don't remember the boys being singled out or punished. The painful part of the story is not what my cousins may or may not have done to me, but that in front of everybody I was hurriedly put into that tub and scrubbed viciously by my mother. It makes sense now, in light of the allegation that my mother may have been raped by her stepfather. The pain of that "washing" forever burned itself into my psyche. I was only five years old.

Our little brother, Oscar, was born on March 19, 1958. Mama called him a "giveaway" baby because he was born in the local state-run charity hospital, Huey P. Long Hospital in Pineville. Oscar was beloved by all of us, being the only boy in the family. However, as he grew, he was even more wild and free than Janis and I ever were.

As a toddler and in his early elementary school years, he was a pest of a boy, always picking at Mama or us girls. Oscar had an Opie Taylor quality about him that made it hard to stay mad at him. He was just so darn cute, with his little blondish-brown bangs and freckled nose, that he could get away with the most outlandish things.

No matter how much he pestered Mama, she always seemed to give over to him, defending his obnoxious behavior. He became the thorn in our sides because Mama would scream at the top of her lungs, "Frances Evelyn," or "Janis Marie . . . you better watch your little brother or I'm gonna whip your ass!"

Daddy would rescue us by taking Oscar fishing or hunting. Their trips began when Oscar was just a toddler. Off they would go with Oscar in a striped T-shirt and blue denim overalls—he even wore a little straw hat! He was so adept at fishing, that at the age of five, he caught a bass big enough to come close to pulling him into the water. This pastime became a serious hobby for Oscar as he matured. Hunting and fishing became a passion for him and he outgrew his little-boy antics. Oscar became, as he aged, as mellow and laid back as our father.

Mama didn't spend any more time with Oscar than she did with us girls, but the level of animosity and tension between them was less intense. If we were to have expressed that Mama showed favoritism among us, it would have been toward Oscar. He was an adorable imp of a baby and little boy who stole everyone's hearts. Mama didn't seem to resent Oscar's relationship with Daddy as she did mine and my sisters'. Daddy was devoted to each of us, but it was natural that in our culture he spent more time with Oscar than us girls. Mama never had the same expectations for Oscar that she did for her daughters. However, she did operate in overdrive with manipulation and guilt toward Oscar. We girls came to understand her nature a bit more than he did because we were in her presence more and we were female.

During the mid to late 1950s, Mama's obsessive-compulsive behavior was somewhat apparent but not extreme. It hadn't elevated to the point that anyone considered it unusual.

Daddy added on to our little shotgun house to make it larger as the family started to grow. It was a source of pride for Mama. Apparently, Mama was a "good housekeeper" at that time. This became an emphasized point repeatedly when family members recalled Mama's behavior from the early years.

We were told many times by various family members that you could practically eat off the floors of the small, green house. When she cleaned the house, she did so with conviction. Rather than a commendable trait, as most family members saw it, this was probably the first noticeable sign of her condition, the rigid preoccupation and perfection in the way she performed tasks. Things had to be cleaned the "right way" or she became exceedingly agitated or angry. Water used to rinse dishes had to be scalding hot, and extra water was added to the ringer-type washer she used for our clothes. She bleached any possible piece of cloth until it eventually became so thin and worn that a child could shred her terrycloth towels into thin strips.

Undoubtedly, the feeling Mama derived from cleaning the house with such precision became for her a soothing ritual that led to a feeling of control over her environment and hence, feelings of familiarity and safety. Originally, there may have been some element of hygiene and a need to scrub away whatever seemed dirty or nasty to her. (She had been whisked away from a dirty old man.) However, this slowly evolved to the creation of an environment solely intended for her self-insulation, whether things were clean or not. This lent the way for her to distance herself emotionally from us children and eventually from my father.

Daddy said even then there was clutter—neat piles of clothing, newspapers, and magazines she would never use or read but kept anyway, using the excuse, "I'm saving these for Pat" (or anybody else who came to mind). As long as she had a reason for keeping anything, she felt justified about stockpiling. Her collecting of unnecessary items would gain momentum as the years progressed.

The late 1950s and early 1960s were probably the most contented years for Mama. Even though she had three small children to care for, she had the love, acceptance, support, and nurturance of Daddy and his extended family, all living in close proximity. In a relatively short period of time she had obtained her dream existence—a new home, a car to drive, a working husband who brought home a paycheck at the end of the week, and money she could spend as she pleased. She had become a part of a connected whole, unlike anything she had experienced in her childhood.

When my paternal grandmother took Mama under her wing, she gave her all she would ever know of genuine motherly love, which my mother so desperately needed. Mama depended on the steadfast care of the old Irish woman. Early on, Mama spent most of her day at my grandmother's house when Daddy was away at work.

Mama also became one of the chauffeurs for the family at large since there weren't many vehicles owned by them. She often took my grandmother on a variety of errands: grocery shopping, doctor appointments, or to pay bills as needed. Mama was accepted, useful, and appreciated.

I'm told that my mother was quite a cut-up and was not afraid to bend the rules. There is a tale about how she drove for years without a driver's license. A state trooper stopped her, and she was ticketed and had to appear in court. Daddy accompanied her. He instructed her to remain relatively quiet, answer questions with a "yes" or "no" and not to offer too much information. He was fearful that the judge would "throw the book at her." Of course, she paid Daddy no attention. The first question she was asked was about the length of time she had been driving with no license. She promptly answered, "Oh, I've been drivin' over three years," in a matter-of-fact tone, as if rules didn't apply to her. Evidently, she hadn't gotten a valid license to drive because she wouldn't have been able to take the written test. Later, Daddy must have asked the Office of Motor Vehicles to allow her to verbally test because from that point on she maintained an up-to-date license.

Mama didn't work outside our home, nor did she want to. Daddy believed it was his responsibility to take care of her and his children. He saw himself as head of household; he was supposed to earn a living for all of us. Besides, as the culture of his day dictated, an upstanding man wanted to be able to have his wife at home with the children. Very early in the '60s, Daddy recognized that Mama was bored. Even though she was able to drive and could go wherever she needed or wanted, she still wasn't quite satisfied with her daily routine.

Daddy bought her a little gift one day, which gave him an idea as to how Mama could stay busy with something besides housework and kids. Alongside some road, a local vendor was selling his wares. Daddy stopped to look at a planter fashioned to resemble a log. The crafty person who made it had used an industrial-sized food can out of which they had cut a large square opening. After covering the tin can with plaster of Paris, they created a bark-like look on the surface using a fork. A short, broken limb was made using aluminum foil wrapped around a small tree limb from the yard, which was covered with the plaster and then attached to the can.

Mama came up with the idea to add a small ceramic bird sitting on either the can or the branch. Once the plaster dried and hardened Mama painted it with wood stain and then she applied a final coat of varnish. Finally, she filled the can with potting soil and planted some type of ivy or mother-in-law's tongue (the *sansevieria* plant). Mama loved the planter and seemed to like the notion of becoming crafty and maybe making some money to boot. Daddy bought the materials for her. A neighbor started supplying her with food cans from the local elementary school and Shirley started helping her assemble the planters. Before long, we had planters everywhere!

Daddy even went so far as to build a small shop next to the house so that Mama could become an entrepreneur of sorts and never have to leave home. She and Shirley started making the planters and soon were making ashtrays and various molded plaster items, which were becoming popular in the area. The shop enjoyed a modest success; however, it was short lived. Mama lost interest when it became work. The shed soon became a place where she could store and pile things up.

Mama evidently had a creative flair, but she never pursued it beyond the making of those planters. I remember her enjoying coloring in coloring books. One of my favorite coloring books as a child was the Walt Disney version of Cinderella. Its pages seemed magical to me; they were precise, pristine, open, and delightful to fill with color. I brought one home with me from my cousin's house once. Mama got it and began coloring.

At first, I was afraid she would mess it up; I wanted to get it away from her. She insisted that she wanted to color and wasn't going to hurt the book. She took a very long time to finish coloring as I impatiently waited, dying to get my own hands on it. It was as if she were an older sister taunting me by not letting me have my turn. I was amazed at the precision she used in coloring the figures. She used the crayon in a way that produced very light, creamy strokes. She stayed in the lines and shaded the images with an intensity I had never seen before. I was probably only seven or eight at the time, but I do recall standing there with my mouth open and my eyebrows raised after she finished—it was beautiful! This was the first indication for me of her perfectionist nature. I just didn't have a clue as to what I was witnessing.

Mama loved to go to Alexandria, roughly twelve miles south of Ball, to get something to eat. Hamburgers were Mama's all-time favorite food. She liked to go to local drive-ins and order them by the sack. There were some places you could actually get a fully dressed hamburger, five for a dollar! Getting hamburgers on the weekend came to be one of our few family outings over the years. Many of the beer joints and local drive-ins featured burgers and fries or curly-ques (curly fries). This was the way most of the people we knew spent their Friday and Saturday nights. This was a big deal outing for the whole family. We usually never went into the establishment. Daddy was the only one to go in, and while he had a few beers, we stayed in the car with Mama and ate our burgers. Many other people were doing the same thing. Over the years, I saw a wide variety of people who socialized in this manner.

Mama wasn't a tiny woman, even though she was short, but she had been "well built" in her teens and early twenties. Many relatives have related to me what a strikingly pretty woman she was in her youth. After Janis and I arrived, she started to gain weight. I suppose pregnancy gave her an excuse to eat whatever she felt like eating. She got progressively heavier as the years passed. Overeating was also another of the first subtle signs of her coping mechanisms.

Later, her eating was almost an act of defiance, especially when she was diagnosed borderline diabetic in her early forties. She would do what she damn well pleased, regardless of the consequences.

Early in one of her pregnancies, probably Oscar, she related to Daddy after her check-up that the "son-of-a-bitch doctor" told her to put a mile of air under her feet every day.

She asked Daddy, "What the hell was that supposed to mean?"

Daddy laughed at Mama's confusion, replying that the doctor meant that it would be good to get some daily exercise. After his explanation Mama retorted, "Aw, he's crazy as hell!"

Daddy began working for Ray Stubblefield, who owned a pest control business based in the small community of Tioga, across the tracks and parallel to Ball. Its main thoroughfare was US 71, which saw much more traffic than did Ball at that time. Ray had a thriving business in the 1950s and throughout the 1960s. Daddy was proud to be a part of that growing service. Times were good; we lived in a new home and had plenty to eat. He was motivated to care for his growing family and to provide for us the things he missed as a child. Mama was well off in comparison to the life she had known before marrying Daddy.

On the weekends, Daddy liked to go to the Palms Drive-In. It was a semifamous beer joint located on Upper Third Street on the northwest side of Alexandria. Daddy went there to have a few beers with his buddies. He had a real Irish gift of gab when he drank. One of his greatest joys in life was to talk politics with whoever had the guts to take him on. He loved to carry on long-winded conversations; few subjects made him uncomfortable. Daddy was one of the most well-read men I knew. He stood inside the small bar area of the drive-in restaurant and talked for hours. Because of the work he did, he knew an incredible number of people around the parish, but then again, he never met a stranger.

Often, Mama and Shirley would accompany Daddy because he didn't drive if he had been drinking. Mama would do the chauffeuring and Shirley would come along to escape country living for a while. Janis and I sat in the back seat of some big, older-model Buick they had during those years, taking turns standing on the hump in the floorboard, peering over the front seat.

Along with Mama and Shirley, we stayed in the car with the windows rolled down so we could hear the jukebox piped from inside into speakers positioned strategically outside on each drive-in stall. The sounds of country and western music, especially Hank Williams, Ernest Tubbs, and Patsy Cline, would fill the night air. Shirley and Mama would sing along, eat their hamburgers, and have a few Tom Collins drinks. I begged for the cherries from their drinks. Mama wouldn't always share, but I could count on Shirley to give me hers. Mama probably only got the drink to make her feel like a grown-up, she had no taste for liquor of any kind.

Mama's mood seemed to me to be considerably light on one of these outings, especially if Daddy had a little money. She loved Fats Domino, so when they played one of his records she would bob her head and purse her red-lipsticked lips in time to the beat. Those were lighthearted, happy times. They just didn't last very long.

Our life on Ball Cut-Off Road could have been the ideal American dream for "regular Joe" people. Essentially, it was the beginning of the suburban life in rural Louisiana. I remember our portion of the road, up to the railroad tracks, when it was gravel and that there were very few houses on it. Toward the end of the 1950s, families were moving out our way to find the peace and tranquility of country life. One of those families bought a red brick spec house, which was built directly across the road from our house. I was about five or six years old.

The Thibodeaux family moved into what we thought of as an uptown abode, with its picture window and single-vehicle covered carport! It was only a small, three-bedroom house, but it was new and had enviable, modern features.

Carmon and Christy were the only two children of Buster and Estelle Thibodeaux and the granddaughters of Trude Rains, Estelle's mother, who lived with them. Buster worked for a local manufacturing company, while Estelle, the first working mother I ever knew, was a nurse's aide at the Baptist Hospital in Alexandria. Neither of them was home during the daytime. They gave strict instructions to My Trude (Christy's pet name for her grandmother that everyone else adopted) that the girls were to stay in the yard.

I'm not sure what those little girls thought they might be finding out in the piney woods of Ball, but Janis and I found a degree of salvation when the "Thibidore" (as Mama pronounced their name) kids moved in. We were more than prepared to show them how kids in the country lived and played.

Our very first encounter with the girls involved the fad for kids that was sweeping the United States at that time, the Hula-Hoop! The evening before, Janis and I had seen them outside. We went to the end of our driveway and waited for them to emerge. They finally came to the edge of their yard next to the ditch but not near the road. They informed us that they couldn't go out of their yard or they would be in trouble. We exchanged names and ages and made a plan to play together the next day. As it was getting near dusk, it wasn't long before their small, hunched-back grandmother, My Trude, called them to come in.

The next morning, Janis and I saw them standing under their carport with their newly acquired hoops, having a good time. Our inherent curiosity and newly acquired jealousy got the better of us even though we were uncertain how the new girls would receive us country bumpkins. We decided to venture across the blacktop anyway to find out what made these new girls tick.

We dressed in our typical, everyday shorts and T-shirts, which may or may not have matched the shorts and were never ironed—play clothes, as Mama called them. We usually went barefoot when the weather was warm.

Janis and I just knew these were city girls because they couldn't cross the road and their manner of dress was much too refined for the way we played. Obviously, they weren't supposed to get their matched outfits and sandals dirty. We had to investigate!

We crossed the road and tentatively approached them as they merrily continued their play, pretending not to notice our arrival. We stood transfixed by their clothes, their house, their toys, and their fun. We felt as if we were on the outside looking in. Little did we know that that day would only mark the beginning of many, many more days of that same gnawing feeling of not quite fitting in with other kids.

Carmon and Christy were just as curious as we were but chose to ignore us for a bit. Finally, they acknowledged our presence. They saw we came empty-handed, but soon they were generous enough to share their pink-and-blue hoops. They just couldn't believe we could cross the road and that we didn't even tell our Mama that we were doing it! Or that the only time we heard from Mama was to keep an eye out for Oscar. They also couldn't believe we were barefoot and didn't own a single Hula-Hoop! We did get a Hula-Hoop later—Daddy made us one out of black PVC pipe.

After a while, Daddy warned us that we were going to wear "our welcome out," and we did, many times over. I'm sure that the O'Neal girls crossing that blacktop road day after day came to be a sight that their whole family dreaded at one time or another. The friendship we forged with them, however, during our childhood, provided a necessary reprieve from abuse and emotional neglect. Janis and I escaped to their home as often as we could and lived vicariously through their lives.

Although at that point we had very little in common, we all knew we would be friends. We traversed the '60s together. We were four little girls who declared our undying love for John, Paul, George, and Ringo. We filled our days by plugging a record player into a long extension cord and dragging it outside so we could play pretend guitars and pantomime the songs of our youth. When young people have a narrow world, they have to enlarge it with big imaginations.

We were four little girls who made mischief together as well as straw playhouses. Making snickerdoodles, eating Popsicles, and watching Ed Sullivan on Sunday nights bonded us like sisters. For Janis and me, life as it could be was framed in Carmon and Christy's front yard on their swing set and in their bedroom, where we rolled our hair with orange juice cans and participated in the slumber parties we couldn't have in our own home. There, we taught each other the latest dances, we did the Twist, and we did the Swim and the Pony and forgot about any troubles waiting at home.

We cried together over bad boys, gossiped about school and the soap operas and longed to see Liverpool. Many of my sunnier '60s memories involved the four of us. For brief moments, Carmon, Christy, Janis, and I were those long-haired, barefoot girls dancing in the moonlight. The only thing that could break us out of one of those reveries was the sound of Mama's voice hollering at us to come see about something she didn't want to deal with.

And so began the making of a mirror that Janis and I would use for a long time to judge our lives. With it, we could gauge whether our reflections came back in any fashion similar to that of the Thibodeaux girls whose lives we so desperately wanted to be ours.

Those whirling hoops have been the markers I have used to denote what might have been. It was the end of our innocent time. The circumstances and situations to come led us down divergent paths, but had they not veered the way they did, would our lives have been much different? I spent way too many years trying to hold on to the hope of what could be and eventually to what might have been. It goes as it goes. You play the hand you are dealt.

Chapter 4

The Fire: We Lost Everything We Owned

Daddy taught me how to read before I entered public school in 1959, and so began Mama's deep-seated resentment of my relationship with Daddy. No longer did she have a willing accomplice in manipulating Daddy into doing her bidding. The toddler parrot that would run into the vegetable garden with Mama's prompting to say, "Daddy, quit working in this ole 'garbage' [garden] and take me and Mama to get a hamburger" was gone. She had been replaced by a sad child who discerned too much of the ways of the adult world.

I watched Daddy closely as he intensely followed world events as reported on television by Chet Huntley and David Brinkley; or watched him faithfully read the *Town Talk*. Those were such serious times. The Bay of Pigs, the Cuban Missile Crisis, and the threat of nuclear war that loomed over our heads unceasingly disturbed him and, in time, disturbed me too. He encouraged me to read anything I could get my hands on, even the back of the cereal box. Because of Daddy, I did read many cereal boxes and much more. Mama blithely existed. Her chief concern was getting her hands on Daddy's paycheck at the end of the week.

When I was about seven years old and in second grade, a series of events began that catapulted Mama into the very dark recesses of her illness, and thus our dark time began as well.

Mama, Marbeth, and Shirley had gone to town (our vernacular for the city of Alexandria) for groceries. They routinely did this together because of the extended family's desire to save money on gas and maintenance for their limited number of vehicles. Daddy and the three of us children were up at Frog's house less than a quarter of a mile northwest through a thicket of pine trees that separated our properties. I don't recall how we all found out that our house was on fire other than that someone passing on Ball Cut-Off Road had seen smoke or flames. I just remember Daddy frantically telling Frog to watch us kids. I watched him disappear as he ran wildly through the pines toward our house.

In our tiny, country community, everybody knew everybody, so people quickly gathered, either to pitch in because there was no local fire department, or to gawk. Mama, Shirley, and Marbeth were on their way back home, traveling the federal highway and approaching Ball Cut-Off Road.

Mama was driving. All three women noticed smoke rising above the line of pine trees as they approached Ball. Instinctively, the two married women remarked that they hoped it wasn't either of their houses. House fires were a common fear for everyone in our community. My uncle Robert told me that Mama knew almost immediately that it was her house burning. He said she became hysterical and started pulling her hair in fear of what was to come.

I must have asked Frog a million questions about what was happening. He patiently tried to calm all of us down. We could see the smoke billowing above the house. I recall being terrified that Daddy would be hurt and that we would have no beds to sleep in that night.

After having to pass the burning house and the line of vehicles stopped on Ball Cut-Off Road, Marbeth somehow got Mama to let her drive them up to her house. They got out of the car, leaving the doors open, sacks of groceries untouched. Mama was hysterical, crying and screaming about the house and the stuff in it.

I remember thinking, *Where's Daddy? Where's Daddy?*

The adults were surrounding Mama, trying to calm her down. "Christine, hush, you're scaring the kids. All that stuff can be replaced!"

She would have none of it. She was wild, aimless in her abandon, arms flailing. She filled the air with curses flung in every direction, but mainly at Daddy, after he came back from trying to extinguish the fire and joined us at his cousin's home.

"Yeah, yeah, they were up here sittin' on their asses, drinkin' beer. He probably left something on the stove and burned my house down!"

These were only some of the statements I remember her making at that time. The hysteria and verbal tirade that followed made the already traumatic experience of the fire seem even worse.

To my childish mind, the whirl of events was confusing and terrifying. *Why would she say that to Daddy? Couldn't she see that he was exhausted and grieving just as we were?*

I thought she would have scratched Daddy's eyes out if she could have gotten away with it. I suppose if people hadn't been restraining her, she might have.

Her frustration and hand-wringing anxiety centered largely on the fact that all the material possessions of her world, her life, were going up in smoke and flame. She was not concerned that her husband and children were possibly hurt or affected by the experience.

The little girl who was so "dirt poor" growing up, who would surreptitiously swallow found nickels or pennies to keep her siblings from getting them and who didn't mind digging through her own shit the next day to retrieve them was once again being hurt. That was the woman-child standing before God and everyone else that day, wailing and wailing her song of pain and loss.

Our house burned to the ground, including the shed. We lost everything we owned. Furniture, appliances, and clothing can be replaced, but not photographs and the memories of a shared life. I mourned for years over a white tulle tutu that had been made for me for a first-grade play. A family friend had sewn multicolored sequins throughout the petals of tulle, and it seemed magical when it flared around my waist.

Daddy took us all down to Maw Maw Linnie's, where we stayed for a while. People were kind; food and clothing soon arrived. I remember their looks of pity when they brought their offerings. I wanted to hide because I felt as if the fire had scarred me in some fashion and those adults could visibly see the nonexistent burns on my body. Our family's trouble was exposed, an embarrassment to me and I think to Daddy as well.

Mama, however, gloried in it. The sympathetic coos and compassionate words of comfort offered by community members, some Mama didn't even know, were like a balm to her seared psychological skin. I watched from my grandmother's kitchen as Mama opened gift boxes, folding back the tissue like an expectant child. She was honing her manipulative skills.

Mama sobbed on cue and thanked the people for their offerings, but in a way that implied we needed more. Our shared family tragedy became personally advantageous for her. Now this hapless child could have others bring those material items she so desperately needed to possess. She would surround herself with those things; they became the arms of comfort no human could ever provide her.

Daddy didn't want to impose his family on Maw Maw Linnie any longer than necessary. A friend of his, Tinker Nugent, lived not far up US Highway 165 on Burma Road. He was a hard-working man like Daddy with a large family to care for. He had a small house next door to his family home, so he kindly offered us a place to stay for a time until we could make other arrangements. We were probably there only over the course of half a school year.

Daddy's brother Ray, hearing of our plight, offered us his home off Ball Loop less than two miles southwest of us on a little dirt road called Clines Road. Since he worked away from the area, he and his wife, Helen, offered their unoccupied house to us. We lived there for about a year, as I recall.

It was a very isolated, pastoral location, but the perfect place to heal after our traumatic loss. Janis, Oscar, and I saw it as a vast playground to explore, but Mama didn't like it. She much preferred the presence of people at that time. I think Daddy probably would have been content to stay there indefinitely. He loved to garden and was quite good at it. Here, he had a large garden and animals he couldn't have on Ball Cut-Off Road.

Long-necked, beautiful—but mean—white geese patrolled the yard, acting as sentries to warn us of approaching strangers or to keep us kids from going where we didn't belong. There was vast pastureland behind the property where cows kept the tall grass down. We climbed through strands of barbed-wire fence to roam the pasture with Daddy. Sometimes we would go down to a branch of Flagon Creek, where it was cool and shady. On breezy fall evenings, the pasture was wonderful. We could see goldenrod or black-eyed Susans as far as the eye could see. Mama, however, didn't share in our love for nature. She pressured my father to get her back to Ball Cut-Off Road so she could be around people again. She wanted to know what was happening with the rest of the family.

Another factor that may have contributed to her discomfort with Uncle Ray's big, old, rambling house was that it wasn't hers to do with as she pleased. Mama couldn't collect and hoard there the way she wanted to because someone else in the family may have commented on it. She had to adhere to an unwritten code of decency regarding the use of another woman's home.

It took some time, but Daddy eventually moved an older house on to our property to replace our burned-out home. He had it renovated with a new roof, interior walls, and floors. Daddy had an environmental sort of mind-set and the idea of building a brand new structure didn't seem practical to him. It was just as well; I can't imagine what my mother would have done with a new home and more space to fill.

Because he was so content at his brother's home, we didn't move into the replacement home right away. He decided to rent it out for a while to make some extra money. Even this was not satisfactory to Mama, who constantly complained about the renters being in her house. After Mama's continual badgering, he finally moved us to the renovated house.

My mother became pregnant with my youngest sister, Kitty, late in 1960. Marbeth Rayner shared with me that she didn't believe Mama actually realized she was pregnant. She never discussed the pregnancy with her.

Kitty was born on September 2, 1961, at the Baptist Hospital. Estelle Thibodeaux still worked there and helped attend to Mama. Kitty's birth coincided with our move into the renovated replacement home on the old homesite.

Kitty was a big-eyed, dark-haired, beautiful baby. Her given name is Katherine Elaine, which is a lovely name. Oscar, however, didn't take to it very well. He took it upon himself to rename our baby sister, "Kitty Sue." That name became her moniker throughout her childhood.

The morning Maw Maw Linnie died was an Indian summer day, September 3, 1962, one year and one day after Kitty was born. Daddy, Mama, Janis, Oscar, Kitty, and I had gone to her house to take Maw Maw Linnie to her doctor's appointment. Later, Daddy recalled that she lingered that morning over minor preparatory chores before leaving. She asked Mama to put Kitty, who was asleep, on her bed. She rubbed the baby's head for a while. She took an exceptionally long time to give herself a sponge bath. After that, she asked Mama to help her dress. All the while, Daddy and we kids waited on the porch.

Daddy was anxious and unusually impatient for his mother to hurry up. He must have wanted to get her to the doctor as quickly as he could. He later said he believed his mother knew it was her time to go. He thought she had deliberately stalled so that she could die in peace at her home.

That is exactly what she did. Daddy walked into her room to check on her progress. He and Mama witnessed her placing her hand over her heart, uttering a small cry and then easing onto the bed. Daddy knew immediately that she was gone. Ever the protector, he wouldn't let us enter the house. He didn't want us to remember Maw Maw Linnie that way.

I distinctly remember my father's manner of grieving. He paced the entire grounds surrounding his mother's home so we wouldn't see him weeping in sorrow.

Cousin Shirley, always so tenderhearted, was deeply affected by her aunt Linnie's passing. She volunteered to watch us kids during the time of the funeral. I think she made the offer in order to shield herself and us from the sadness of Maw Maw Linnie's death. From our grandmother's front porch we watched the long line of automobiles processing along the Ball Cut-Off Road. The line moved slowly past the O'Neal-Rayner property out of respect for one of the most humble women the community of Ball had known. She was buried in the Springhill Cemetery where her other family members had been laid to rest.

These two images are symbolic for me of intense grief. I will never forget them. For with my grandmother's passing also went any chance for respite from the storms that lay ahead.

Chapter 5

He Could Feel the Larvae Moving through His Bloodstream

When my father worked for Ray's Pest Control, he made a decent salary. He didn't have to contemplate asking Mama to work away from home. His belief was that a man took care of his wife and children. Those prosperous years were very important to him and Mama as well. This was her little piece of status she could hold over her sisters and mother. They could envy her life as being better than theirs was.

My family settled into the renovated house, which we called the new house. There, we tried to adjust to Maw Maw Linnie's passing and the loss of our former home. Life looked as if it might regain some sort of normalcy, but then another tragedy struck. My father was exposed to a very rare and odd situation as a pest control agent.

Daddy and the other men he worked with had to crawl under houses to treat them for termites. Most of the houses in our area at the time were wood-frame homes set on pier-and-beam foundations. There were very few homes in our community built of brick, which usually had solid, concrete slab foundations.

Another common factor during those days was that dogs were allowed to roam free on a person's property, hence the term, yard dogs. Most folks didn't kennel their dogs; they simply used an old shed or doghouse in the backyard for shelter. Because it's so unbearably hot in Louisiana in the summer, many of these dogs took refuge under their owner's home, where they would dig out a place to lay in the cool soil, out of the broiling sun.

Ticks and fleas are quite prolific around these parts, but few people knew about an equally prolific mite that lived in the fur of animals. During certain times of the year, the mites would lay their eggs in the same cool soil where the dogs made their beds. When the mite eggs hatch, they release a microscopic larva that isn't detectable by the human eye.

As my father and his partner crawled through those beds, they were unaware that they were being exposed to thousands of the larvae. Weeks after their exposure, what they thought was heat rash on their upper bodies became a full-blown patch of angry, red flesh. My father was being treated with injections of cortisone for the itching rash by an old dermatologist in Alexandria.

While working in Alexandria one afternoon, Daddy and the other man, who was elsewhere at the time, had what appeared to be a heart attack about thirty minutes apart. My father had an idea about what might have been happening. Since he was near the dermatologist's office, he went there and the doctor treated him with more cortisone. Physicians admitted my dad's partner to the local hospital and treated him for myocardial infarction.

This was the beginning of a living hell for my father. He said he could literally feel the larvae move through his bloodstream. The itching and swelling were unbearable. This condition took a tremendous toll on Daddy physically and emotionally.

Daddy was a beer-drinking Irishman who usually couldn't tolerate hard liquor. The worst night of this condition caused him to ask Mama to go to town to get him a pint of whiskey. I vividly remember him downing that bottle. Afterwards, he laid a wet towel over his bare chest and stood in front of a box fan placed on a kitchen chair. This was the only way he could get some relief from the intolerable sensation he felt in his body. The liquor made him pass out for the rest of the night.

The next morning Daddy asked Mama to drive him to the VA emergency room located in Pineville. The medical staff there admitted him. Later, the VA physicians transferred him to the VA in Shreveport, Louisiana. We were told that Daddy had a nervous breakdown and would be in the hospital for quite a while. This was an unbelievable blow to all of us. Daddy had no medical leave with his job. His income, which supported our household, just stopped. It seemed as though overnight we had become completely destitute.

I think my mother actually held up well for that duration of time. She was getting a great deal of sympathy and petting from everyone, especially her family. They were quick to tell her how to get whatever assistance she could from various places. She managed to sign up for welfare and food stamps for the five of us, because Daddy was in the hospital. This was a shameful thing for Janis and me to deal with, but Mama seemed to handle it very well. What she considered as getting something for nothing came very naturally for her. Daddy was in the hospital for four long months. That time seemed like an eternity to us kids.

I don't remember much of what transpired during his time away from home. But I do recall how thin and pale he was when he did return. My sister Kitty was a very small infant. During Daddy's convalescence, he mainly took care of her. He often said that he had her talking at seven months (which may not have been an exaggeration!).

I learned a long time later that the physicians originally thought the larvae would surround Daddy's heart, affecting the heart's ability to pump blood, which would eventually lead to his death. Daddy had been released from the hospital with a terminal prognosis. He hadn't been told in Shreveport. His records were forwarded to his family physician, who supposedly had the responsibility of letting Daddy know. Dr. Murrell, who Daddy respected immensely, agreed with Daddy that man could never be certain as to the time anyone had left on this earth. Daddy believed a person's mortality was in the hands of "the man upstairs." Because of the prognosis, Daddy was able to obtain Social Security disability benefits.

Grueling months passed before he was approved. I remember that we all felt the tremendous pinch of poverty during those terrible days. Our electricity was turned off for a while. We used coal-oil lamps to light our home. We did have gas for the stove and hot water heater, and the waterworks district never shut the water off.

The nights were very quiet and solitary. Janis and I would lie on a bed and make "shadows" on the wall by raising our arms in the light of the lamp to entertain ourselves. Daddy would sometimes fry potato "chips" for us by thinly slicing fresh potatoes and then deep-fat frying them until they were very crisp. We felt very poor because we couldn't even afford to buy a bag of "store-bought" potato chips.

School was particularly humiliating. I was in fourth grade at that time. We didn't have the money to purchase the school supplies and necessary workbooks I needed at Paradise Elementary. I remember explaining that my daddy had been sick so I didn't know when I could bring the money to pay for my workbooks.

My teacher was a kind, gentle-spirited woman. She said that I would have a special desk to sit at so I could store the materials I needed for school. It was like a miniature office desk with filing drawers on the side that locked. I truly did think I was special because none of the other kids had a desk like it.

When I told Daddy about it, he looked at me quizzically and asked several questions. He didn't say anything else to me about the incident. The next day I was in a regular desk. Years later, I learned that he had gone to the school the next day, furious!

He told my principal, Mr. White, "You son of a bitch, how dare you separate my child from everyone else because I can't afford to pay for her supplies! I won't have you shaming her because of my shortcomings!"

Mr. White wasn't a bad person, I'm sure he and my teacher were trying to act as good stewards of tax dollars. But, like his mama, Linnie, Pat O'Neal wasn't going to allow his children to be shamed for something they couldn't help.

My mother seemed calm at this time. I suppose that with Daddy being home and having someone to help her with an infant while the rest of us were in school, she wasn't overwhelmed. The thought that her husband might die may not have taken on for her the gravity it might have for some other young women. I know she was impatient about the financial situation, but she did know that there was light at the end of the tunnel.

She nagged him relentlessly about when he would start receiving benefits. She also had an uncanny ability to filter and store information that would prove useful to her in some future respect. Somewhere in her mind, a seed was probably taking hold. That thought allowed her to believe that if he did die, she would be entitled to widow's benefits, and the four of us children would receive benefits as his dependents.

I am truly thankful that it didn't come to that. Daddy's body eventually rejected the larvae. The body is such an awesome machine in that it has the ability at times to protect itself. It must have been a horrible experience to cough out tiny invaders from the lungs and pass them through the regions of the bowels. That's how Daddy's system defended itself. This process left him physically weak and virtually shell-shocked. His nerves would never be the same again.

Chapter 6

The Slow, Methodical Steps to Hoarding

Once Daddy's Social Security checks started coming in, we all breathed a collective sigh of relief. Because there was an income again, we could believe that things would be okay. Life had resumed in an almost humdrum way. The fights and arguments common between Mama and Daddy before he got sick were not as frequent. Maw Maw Linnie's death and Daddy's illness had a sobering effect on everyone.

Looking back, it's apparent that the preceding events were the stepping-stones for Mama's leap into the murky depths of obsessive-compulsive hoarding disorder. Slowly, methodically, Mama began collecting all the things she thought she needed to replace after the fire. Nothing was culled. The excuse of the fire remained a viable one in her thought processes far longer than necessary.

At first, it was knickknacks, "Oh, I had one of these," Mama would say when we went to a store. Whether or not that was true made no difference. She couldn't turn anything down that she associated with having been lost in the house fire. She frequented thrift stores and discount outlets. Every visit to one of her sisters or her mother yielded some new treasure they might have wanted to get rid of.

Many times we would actually go to the Pineville city dump with her sister Claudie and her kids and dig through the refuse there. The smell of the smoldering piles from the daily landfill burns would fill our noses, clothes, and hair as we scoured the vast, flat acreage for loot on late Sunday afternoons. To this day the smell of creosote (which is produced in Pineville) late in the evening reminds me of those embarrassing jaunts. There we were, a whole carload of kids hanging out the windows with two crazy women on our way to dig in garbage!

Aunt Claudie was Mama's source for much more than household items and trinkets. She and her husband, Buddy, who was deaf, lived in a huge, fine, old, three-story Victorian house on the riverfront in the city of Pineville. The house had probably been a showplace in its heyday but was in considerable disrepair when Claudie's family lived there. The house always needed painting. The wide front concrete steps were cracked and crumbly in spots and the expansive wooden porch had areas of rotting boards that creaked and sunk if you stepped on the wrong ones. Even as a kid, I was fascinated by the house.

I hated going to Claudie's because I didn't particularly care for her, but I loved the house. As children, we were relegated to the yard to "play" with Claudie's three boys and her daughter. There were enormous, old magnolias in the yard whose limbs heavily drooped due to their large, dark-green leaves and huge seedpods. Because of the amount of shade produced by the trees and the lack of nutrients in the soil, there wasn't any grass growing close to the house. We were left to devise a pastime of playing on the gnarly roots of the trees or digging in the dirt.

Their yard was filled with old broken-down vehicles, broken bikes, rabbit and chicken cages, squawking guinea hens, and various piles of junk-iron and wheels gathered by Uncle Buddy and the boys. I remember a *Family Circus* cartoon from the '60s featuring an outdoor scene. The cartoonist, Bill Keane, drew so many things going on in it, I thought he must have seen the Isaac home and used it as a model for his art.

Mama and Claudie generally stayed in the house drinking coffee and gossiping about everyone they knew and some they didn't know. The two of them cooked up many offenses against other family members and acquaintances. Maw Maw Lavinia had taught them well. They didn't need to venture out into the world to accomplish their evil mischief. The telephone was their weapon of choice. They liked to get people in trouble; anything was fair game, from ratting out some philandering spouse to making false reports of food stamp or welfare fraud, it didn't matter to them. If it appeared that someone was doing better than they were, then they had to cause that person some grief.

It was no wonder that as Claudie's kids grew, they took on some of that behavior. A couple of her boys liked to sit on Maw Maw Lavinia's front porch to watch the repercussions of their mischief making. They would pull the old rotary phone with its long cord outside with them. They loved to call the police or an ambulance to the home of an innocent neighbor just to stir things up when they got bored. They laughed and cackled hysterically watching the unsuspecting neighbor get dressed down by the service agency who answered the call.

Compared to Mama, Claudie was slim, petite, and reasonably well kept. Claudie favored Maw Maw Lavinia in looks and temperament. She teased and styled her bottle-blond hair and applied harsh make-up and drawn-on eyebrows if she was going to town. Otherwise, she more often kept slim brush rollers in her hair most of the day, covered by a thin, mesh hairnet. She was coarse (even her voice) and slightly crude, and she could be despicably mean to some people, including her children, just like her mama, Lavinia. She scared me.

I don't think she was ever overtly mean to my siblings or me, especially if Daddy was anywhere near. But she always questioned us. I felt as though she thought we were trying to put on airs because we didn't behave the way she or her children did. Much was made over the fact that we liked to read or that we did well in school. This set us apart from them. It was as though she wanted us to trip up and do something bad. It also seemed that if she or her kids could have made that happen, they would have taken great delight in seeing one of us fall.

Claudie had an ever-present cigarette in her hand, and through the smoke she would stare at us. She had the annoying habit of saying "uh-huh" to every response we might offer, as if she was seriously considering what we said. She was actually looking for valuable information she could potentially use. I felt a huge element of distrust toward her. She reminded my sister Kitty of a witch. She wasn't illiterate, like Mama. She probably had gone somewhat further in school than Mama did. She was undereducated, ignorant about some subjects, but she was not stupid. She reigned over her domain like an ice queen. Her three sons and one daughter were just as enigmatic as she was. On the surface, they appeared to be ignorant rednecks, but they somehow knew how to operate in the world by their own sets of rules.

Daddy often said that the parish authorities should erect a twelve-foot hurricane fence around the property to keep them away from the rest of the world. They did live in their own universe. Although Claudie rarely left the "compound," she knew everything that was going on because she was a prolific telephone user. Also, from early on her boys roamed the streets of Pineville bringing back local news and gossip they thought their mother could use.

The two most sympathetic people in this maddeningly curious group were Uncle Buddy and his slightly retarded brother, Sonny Boy. Uncle Buddy lost his hearing after a childhood bout of meningitis. I think Uncle Buddy got lucky with that hearing loss; he smiled continually. He would nod his head at one of us before happily going about his business. Uncle Buddy never had to hear the redneck cacophony coming from Claudie and the kids. It was amazing to see the way they communicated with him for they had devised their own form of sign language. Even the baby girl caught on quickly to the signs, so she too could get her father to understand.

Uncle Buddy drove a garbage truck for a living. Sonny Boy rode shotgun. Uncle Buddy had contracted as an independent hauler of refuse such as boxes and paper goods from the Alexandria/Pineville city merchants. Claudie had trained him and Sonny Boy well. They were to bring home anything that might appear valuable or usable to add to her own eclectic mix of treasures.

When you entered their home, it was clean, neat, and organized, but it was like entering a macabre museum. The discarded, cracked, broken, or misshapen articles and fixtures rescued from behind some store were the furnishings on display in every room. There was a gorgeous, crystal chandelier in the living room that, even to my untrained eye, was inappropriate. Its sparkle and shine still attracted me.

I would stand open-mouthed, viewing it from underneath. My careful observation soon revealed that there were many missing teardrop crystals around the lamp's circumference. Almost everything in the house was like that, even the food.

Uncle Buddy sometimes retrieved produce along with the boxes he picked up. Not only were the eyes accosted by the bizarre interior, but the nose as well. There was always a lingering, pungent aroma of fruits and vegetables in various stages of ripeness or rotting that wafted through the house.

My first experience with exotic (for us) fruits like grapefruit, coconuts, and pineapples came from the Isaac home. Mama would never purchase such items because they were either too expensive or she had no idea how to prepare them. She would bring them home mainly because they were free and because she knew Daddy had a palate for foods we didn't ordinarily have. Along with the produce, she would sometimes bring outdated boxed food like dried apricots or crackers. Not only did Mama bring home the purloined produce and wacky "whatnots," but she also brought, unknowingly at first, some very nasty little critters we never got rid of: the small German roach.

Daddy warned her repeatedly that we didn't need the stuff. He told her every cardboard box and paper bag she brought into our house was a potential time bomb waiting to explode in our faces. She ignored his warnings even though he was an expert in the field of pest control. She continued sneaking boxes and bags into the house.

Later, when Daddy's patience wore thin and he had a few beers under his belt, he would chastise her in a sarcastic tone about how she and her "little friends," the roaches and rats, were taking us over. More often than not, she would get mad and cuss him out, but she never heeded his well-intentioned lecture. It shamed him that his children were living in a house infested with roaches. He could never eliminate that infestation completely because Mama had to fulfill her need for things.

None of the gathering and collecting happened suddenly. This was a gradual process. Over time, it was to become exceedingly worse. Her behavior was manageable to a degree. Daddy would fuss when the house got exceedingly dirty but he didn't begrudge her having things. That wasn't his nature. She would clean up a bit or pick things up to appease him, but he wasn't hardcore about the house being spotless. She was still cooking and washing our clothes and sheets, enough to get by.

Already, our family unit wasn't encouraging visitors to our home. The few family members like Shirley and Uncle Wig or the Thibodeaux girls, who came on a regular basis, became accustomed to Mama's collecting, just as we had. The hoarding was becoming more obvious. Only later would it become the all-consuming purpose for her existence. None of us knew what we were experiencing. Nobody ever used the term obsessive-compulsive hoarder.

Chapter 7

Mama and the Silver-Foil Christmas Tree, Bridal Wreath Switches, and Delaware Punch

Mama's other behavioral characteristics were obvious to us because they became sources of embarrassment or frustration on the part of all of us. Chief among them was her extreme jealousy. Many of the arguments she and Daddy had were rooted in that acidic emotion. It ate away at her and drove her at the same time. She always had to know where Daddy was, whom he was with, how much money he had, or how much money he had spent. With every question spoken aloud or not, her anxiety rose. When her anxiety rose, somebody had to pay for it, usually us kids. She would take her ire out on anybody within her reach. Her rage was terrible to behold.

Once she sailed a gaudy ceramic ashtray across the living room after Daddy pissed her off about something. No one could remember what the argument was about or even what prompted it. But we all remembered her rage and its aftermath. The ashtray clipped Daddy on his forehead, right above the eye, and gave him an ugly gash, which bled profusely. All of us kids screamed and cried at the sight of the blood running down his face, but Mama showed no remorse. She muttered under her breath that it served him right. He had not behaved the way she thought he should have.

Her black-and-white way of thinking allowed no gray to enter. Either it would be done the way she thought it needed to be done, or there would be hell to pay. That black-and-white thinking dominated every aspect of almost every relationship she had.

Another aspect of Mama's character was her lack of compassion. Mama never showed us kids much in the way of compassion, understanding, or patience. She seemed to endure us. For the most part, it seemed as though we were her possessions, something to be used as she desired. Daddy insisted we respect her because she was our mother. And we did, but it was sometimes hard to do so. If she showed any kindness, it was usually solicitous. There was always a price tag with her niceties; she wanted something for it. We could always tell when she wanted something or was being manipulative because she would speak in the third person. "Mama needs you to do" such and such, or "Mama sure would like a cold drink, go down to the [gas] station and get me one." She was famous for calling one of us "baby" when she particularly tried to convince us of something. She never used that sweet tone during a regular day.

I was terrified of getting injections when I was a child. Everything about a doctor's office frightened me. Once I entered the building, and the antiseptic, alcohol smell and the sterile look of the rooms accosted my senses, my bottom lip started quivering immediately. I would become physically ill with fright.

Once I had to get an injection for tonsillitis when I was quite young. After a round of uncontrollable crying and trembling, the poor nurse was able to give me the "shot," but not because Mama had made me feel more at ease. She was not sympathetic. The nurse finished and told me I could go. I limped out of the exam room because not only was my butt throbbing, but also I was still petrified and wanting sympathy. The nurse asked if there was something wrong and Mama quickly responded, "Oh, don't worry about her, she's just puttin' on!" With that, she grabbed me by the arm and yanked me impatiently toward the door.

The only time I can remember being sick to the point of vomiting (as a child) was once when I was about seven. I had fever and chills and was terribly nauseated, probably from a bad ear infection. I was on the couch feeling miserable. Shirley happened to be visiting that evening. Someone gave me 7UP to drink, but I couldn't keep it down, and I vomited. Mama didn't come to see about me; instead, Shirley held me until I was finished. She got a washcloth, cleaned my face, and comforted me while I cried. She then held me until I felt better. I remember her act of kindness and compassion to this day. Shirley's simple act of kindness was something only Daddy gave to me in our household.

Daddy was the disciplinarian; Mama was the abuser. For the most part, she would scream or cuss at us as her form of discipline. We stayed out of her reach because if she went into one of her rages and was close by, she might haul off and hit one of us. On occasion, she would take a belt, a switch from a bridal wreath (spirea) bush in the yard, or a hairbrush to us as her weapon of choice. I don't recall any of us ever doing anything that was worthy of being striped with a belt or switch, but that was how she dealt with us.

A few years ago, I watched the video of the movie, *Divine Secrets of the Ya-Ya Sisterhood*. Having read Rebecca Wells's book, I could identify with the characterization of the family in the story. A particular scene in which the mother beats her children especially resonated with me.

The children were playing on their front porch and then went out into their yard in the middle of a downpour. The mother came out into the rain after them, striking them repeatedly with a belt. Although I had read the book and remembered that segment, I could not have prepared myself for the intensity of Ashley Judd's portrayal. Almost immediately, I broke down and wept uncontrollably. I had to leave the room. I'm sure my poor husband thought I had lost it! The scene was like an unexpected replay of my childhood. For a moment, I felt as though I was watching myself and my siblings go through the exact experience. *What was I remembering?*

It then occurred to me that Mama had once caught us on the flat roof of an addition to the back of our house we referred to as the "drop room." At first she screamed at us that she was "gonna beat our asses" for being up there. Because we didn't want to be hit, we ignored her and didn't come down (we knew she wouldn't climb up). She went around to the front of the house for a minute and then came back to the corner and peered around, saying in a voice dripping with honey, "Ya'll can come down now." We asked for assurance that she wasn't going to whip us, and she said she wouldn't.

Janis, Oscar, and I slowly backed off the roof and started descending the ladder to the cushiony grass below. Mama had silently crossed the distance from the corner of the house across that thick carpet of St. Augustine grass without us hearing her. As soon as Janis's foot hit the ground, Mama was on her with a large switch off the bridal wreath bush from the front yard.

I remember our screams because she was on us like a mad dog. She began striking out and striking out as we tried to get away from her. She held one of us by the arm, and with her free arm she struck repeatedly at the other two because she could. She had us cornered like animals.

If we didn't deal with outright abuse from her, then we had to contend with her manipulative behavior. When we got older, she would purposely let us skip school on the third of the month when Daddy's disability check came in so someone would be with her when she got the check cashed. She would promise us something if we skipped school. She didn't want to go to the bank or other places to pay bills alone. Mama would say "those people" were going to "gyp" her out of her money. She didn't trust people to give her the correct amount of money at the bank or the right change back when she paid a bill or bought groceries.

If we told her no, because something important was going on at school, she would insist we go. She would raise hell at us until we relented; other times, she bribed us with some new jeans or a hamburger or something so she wouldn't have to deal with the situation alone. The trip to town was always an ordeal because she would stay at the bank's drive-through or in a checkout line longer than necessary. Whoever was with Mama had to count the money a couple of times, with her prompting us to "make sure that's right!"

Some of the more embarrassing experiences with Mama had to do with our car, a long, slim Chevrolet station wagon painted a noxious color that Mama called "titty pink." The car stalled almost every time we stopped for a traffic light. If there was no man around for Mama to flag down and then sweet talk into jump-starting the car, then she would make Janis and me get out and push the car until she could get it cranked again.

If any man did stop to help and asked us how far away we lived, Mama's infamous reply was always "Oh, just over yonder on Balls Cut-Off Road" (with a heavy emphasis on making Ball plural). Janis and I never knew the greater offense to our pride—was it to be forced to humiliate ourselves on a public thoroughfare, or was it to hear our mother flirt with and then manipulate complete strangers into coming to her rescue?

Mama didn't limit her verbal or physical assaults to our immediate family. She was usually quite physically healthy, although she got progressively stouter in girth. She was rarely ill and was physically strong. She could take on a man without blinking an eye. Uncle Wig was small and wiry like Grandpa Frazier. He liked to tilt his bottles of port wine a wee bit as well. Mama mostly despised him. She had neither sympathy nor tolerance for any of his inebriated antics.

He lived like a hermit in my grandmother's house after she died. He let all the utilities be turned off, which required him to use coal-oil lamps, well water, and a wood-burning stove for his personal needs. Although he was eccentric and reclusive, he never intentionally hurt or bothered anyone.

Once he came to our house about midmorning, pretty well looped, looking for Daddy, who wasn't home that particular day. The liquor had loosened his tongue and he got mouthy with Mama about how mean she was to everybody. They had a little "tête-à-tête" right there in the kitchen.

The next thing you know, "Chrissie" had him by the seat of his overalls and the scruff of his neck, and out the screen door, across the back porch, and into the yard he flew.

"Get your ass on down the road, Wig O'Neal, or I'm gonna put my foot where the sun don't shine, you dried-up little bastard!" Mama shouted at him as he staggered back down the trail. It was a while before he came back to our house.

They finally worked out a sort of truce because Uncle Wig perpetually needed a way to go to town for groceries or hooch. Mama was usually home and Daddy kept her supplied with some old, used vehicle or another. By that time, she had been taxiing Wig and other family members to town for years. Mama expected them to pay dearly for the service. She did nothing out of the goodness of her heart—a person owed her no matter how long it took.

She made a point of being available on payday or the first or third of the month when veteran's benefits or Social Security checks came in, because someone inevitably needed a way to go to the bank. She knew that once they got a few beers or wine in their gut, she could more easily get a few bucks out of them. Sometimes, if they passed out in the car, she would even roll them for whatever money was loose in their pants pockets. This made Daddy bitterly angry if he caught her.

Like her sister Claudie and their mother, Mama was nosy as hell. Gossip was her main form of entertainment. She absolutely wore telephones out! She never seemed interested in communicating with anyone unless there was some element of "getting the dirt" on someone else. She didn't read the newspaper and rarely watched television, except for the soaps, but she knew all the latest on most of the people living in Ball. This poisonous gossip became a root cause of many arguments between her and Daddy. He abhorred her lengthy phone diatribes about family members or acquaintances. No amount of chastisement or pleading could prevent the behavior.

Most of the gossip was centered on Mama's intense jealousy of others' acquisitions. A family considered well off in our neighborhood, compared to everyone else, got much of Mama's attention. This was because they got new vehicles frequently and had a nice, big brick home.

The year the silver-foil Christmas trees with their accompanying revolving colored lights came out, Mama was positively at her peak with jealous gossip. The enchanting tree with its pink bulbs and glowing lights glittered through the neighbor's big picture window.

Mama and Shirley had driven into Pineville to get eggnog from a fast food dairy barn. The eggnog was mixed with soft-serve ice cream and sold in a cardboard gallon container. The heat from the car made the mixture a little soupy. As Mama turned on Ball Cut-Off Road, in the darkness of that early December evening, she couldn't take her eyes off the Christmas tree. She was so caught up in envy that she wasn't watching the road and ended up in the ditch. Poor Shirley, who had been holding the eggnog, ended up with the sticky mess all over her head and lap!

One of the few ongoing relationships Mama had over the years was with Lee Rayner, wife to Frog's brother, Willard "Bitty." She and Mama bonded quickly in an intensely toxic relationship.

She was one of the most mean-spirited women I ever knew. She and Bitty were complete opposites. He was a kind-hearted person with an affable, lopsided grin. He loved to laugh. Bitty had traveled a bit while serving in the navy before returning to Ball to live. He met Lee while stationed in Florida and married her prior to his return to Louisiana. Lee had been married before and had three sons who Bitty accepted as his own.

When Bitty brought Lee and her boys back home to live on Rayner property, they were the talk of the community. Lee initially put on her best behavior, but most people felt put off by her Yankee accent and her coarse mannerisms. Mama and Lee had similar physical builds and temperaments.

Both were hefty, big-boned women with olive complexions and dark, wavy hair.

Lee talked through the side of her mouth in a barroom brawl sort of way, sometimes with her cigarette hanging out the corner of her mouth. She accepted no backtalk from her boys or Bitty, either. Nobody in the family called him Willard, except Lee. She was notorious for making comments about how she told "Willard Rayner" how things were going to be—she ruled that house of men like an iron-fisted drill sergeant.

Daddy absolutely despised her. He cared about his cousin deeply and he couldn't stand to see Bitty have to kowtow to this hateful woman. He wasn't especially thrilled when Mama and Lee hooked up and became good gossip buddies and traveling companions. They would connive together to cause trouble for others in the family by spreading malicious half truths, making innuendos, and giving out much too much information. Both of them were so devoid of any kind of productive activity or emotions that their malignant talk and meanness became a sick form of entertainment for them.

Lee loved to give Mama advice about how she needed to handle Daddy or her kids. I remember her saying in her gruff voice, "Welllll, Chris, if I were you, I'd whip their asses all over this place. No kid of mine is gonna tell me nothin' and that old man of yours would have his ass out doin' somethin' besides [whatever Mama might have been griping about on any given occasion]." Between the two of them, they stirred up trouble and misery for everyone in the family.

Mama and Lee liked to get things at a bargain. They started going to stores and garage sales together. Soon, they developed a reputation for their bargaining and their downright harassment of a person regarding the value of an item. Nobody wanted to be in their company because they were so embarrassing.

Mama's relationship with Lee empowered her to become more verbally abusive toward all of us. She adopted many of Lee's mannerisms, stabbing the air with a cigarette for emphasis. After all, if Lee could do it and get away with it, why couldn't she? Their twisted relationship was the source of many arguments between Daddy and Mama and others in the family. Once she and Lee became buddies, Mama lost some favor with Daddy's relatives who had previously been slightly sympathetic toward her. They lost patience and trust in dealing with her.

Mama was displaying a greater sense of herself. The relationship with Lee seemed to infuse her with a sense of greater power. The arguments between my parents were heightened at this time. Mama seemed driven to gain more and more possessions regardless of what anyone thought. Daddy was staying away from home more, and my siblings and I found every opportunity possible to stay away as well.

I didn't like to be around my mother; she embarrassed me. The way she acted was far removed from how I thought a mother should be. I couldn't trust her as an important adult in my life. It seemed as though she was going to do whatever she pleased, regardless of any responsibility she owed her family.

A characteristic that was more than difficult for me to deal with was Mama's greed. Daddy would have, as the old cliché goes, given someone the shirt off his back. This wasn't the case with my mother. She always operated out of a spirit of "never enough." Even if she couldn't use something or if it was perishable and would eventually rot, she still wouldn't get rid of it. She might need it one day.

Sharing was not a virtue or even a thought in Mama's mind. I think she believed that if she was separated from one of her possessions, a part of her was being taken. Little did I know then that obsessive-compulsive hoarders often feel that way about their possessions.

We used to be amazed and laugh at how fast she could down a bottle of cold Delaware Punch or a Nehi orange. This was an outward expression of that need she had to consume and to hoard. To keep others from the things she wanted. She didn't even want to share with her children unless there was something in it for her.

Much, much later, when the hoarding was at its peak, I discovered a full box of Hubba Bubba bubble gum in her home. When I asked her why she had bought the gum, which she could no longer chew because all her teeth had been pulled, she said it was for Oscar's son, Shawn. The sad truth was that she would never give the gum to her grandson. He was just a convenient excuse for the purchase of a case of gum, which only candy vendors would have bought! We never knew the motivations or thoughts that drove her to obtain things, and therein lay some of our frustration. Her actions seemed devious, mean spirited, and hateful.

Chapter 8

The Breakdown: She Put a "Do Not Disturb" Sign

on Her Soul

The small measures of longed-for peace after Daddy's hospitalization and subsequent return home didn't last long. The promise of stability seemed just over the horizon. Then Mama took the big dive.

We still were not out of the woods financially, which left Mama constantly fuming, wanting things, and worrying about how to get them. Marbeth and Frog, however, were doing relatively well, even though they had four kids to feed and clothe, as did Mama and Daddy.

The custom of visiting in each other's homes came naturally to the young couples in part because Daddy and Frog were so close. They took turns hosting. On the weekends, the men barbecued chickens and sausage or fried fish, while the women made potato salad, french fries, and hush puppies when we gathered for family outings.

It happened, however, that family members weren't visiting at our house as much as they had previously because they didn't feel comfortable. Usually, we visited in their homes. We had one such outing at Frog's invitation. He and Marbeth had purchased a new TV. They invited us up to spend an evening watching it.

In early 1992, only a few months before Daddy died, we talked about that evening. He believed it was the pivotal moment in time before Mama broke completely. There was no defining trauma, scalding fight, or argument; everyone had gotten along well. We watched the evening's television offerings from the local NBC station. The adults visited and we children played with not a cross word passed between anyone.

When we got back home, my younger siblings and I went to bed. Mama went to the bathroom. Daddy read for a while, before he too went to retire for the evening. He told me he had noticed that Mama had gone to the one bathroom we all shared right after we had gotten in from Marbeth and Frog's house. A short while later he went to their bedroom (they were still sharing a bed at that time). Mama wasn't there. He couldn't figure out why she might still be in the bathroom. He said he considered that she might be taking a bath. He waited for a while; finally, hearing no noise, he thought he had better investigate.

He knocked on the closed bathroom door, which Mama didn't typically close. He called out to her but got no response. Instinctively, he knew something was terribly wrong. He opened the door, not knowing what to expect. He thought she might have passed out, but he didn't expect her to be sitting on the commode staring blankly into space.

Softly, he called, "Christine," but he got no response. Frightened now, he put his hand on her shoulder, slightly shaking her, then more firmly calling, "Christine, Christine, what's the matter?" Still, there was no response. He described her as being catatonic. Somehow, he got her up and into the bedroom without her ever protesting or uttering a sound. Daddy spent a restless night but was ready early the next morning to take her to the hospital.

As Daddy shared his vivid memory with me in my living room in the winter of 1992, I could see the pain and angst he still felt. Bewilderment had tormented him all those years. He, just like his children, had tried to unravel the knots to try to figure out what had happened to Mama. After thinking about every possible reason for her mental breakdown, he had concluded that her monstrous jealousy and greed had finally pushed her full force into her disorder. I sat silently for a long time. It was such an implausible concept, and yet I knew he was probably correct.

I had to ask, even though I knew the answer, "Jealous about what, Daddy?"

He responded, "Because Marbeth got a new TV and she didn't."

There, it was out. She didn't break when her little house burned. She didn't break when the only real mother she ever knew died. She didn't break when her husband nearly died. She didn't break when her four kids went to school in hand-me-downs and giveaways. But she did break over a goddamned television set. What do you make of that? (As my daddy would say.)

It seems as though humans walk a fine line when it comes to making choices. For all the years Mama spent neglected and abused, either by the adults in her childhood who I believe betrayed her and/or because of her life's harsh circumstances, she chose the easiest path available to her. Scream, scream, scream, kick, kick, kick, demand, demand, demand, hit, hit, hit, and if that doesn't work, place the "do not disturb" sign on the door to your soul and go somewhere else. She remained a child and God help us and forgive us because we didn't know how to help her.

This then was the piece I struggled with for so many years and sometimes still do. It was especially difficult for me to come anywhere near understanding where my mother was psychologically. I couldn't wrap my brain around someone needing things over caring about her own family. *Was this a mental illness? Was her condition a by-product of a world gone mad to possess stuff? Or could it have been something darker, uglier, and more malevolent?*

It scared the hell out of me not to know what I was dealing with and what the father I had so dearly loved had had to contend with most of his adult life. Fear and concern wrapped its tentacles around my heart as to how my sisters, brother, and I had been affected by our mother's behavior.

Chapter 9

"Poor Chrissie, Poor Chrissie!"

Daddy got Mama to the hospital as quickly as he could. He called Marbeth to come watch us. She was just as puzzled and alarmed as he was. Mama was committed to Central State Hospital in Pineville. It was the largest mental health facility in the state at one time, a virtual city unto itself. And everybody knew its purpose. Local people frequently peppered their disciplinary threats with phrases like, "If you don't start behavin', you're gonna make me have to go to Central." Central became a word synonymous for the place where crazy people lived. Mama was there for six weeks.

Daddy explained to us kids that Mama's mind was sick and she would need rest. The explanation Daddy got from the hospital's physicians regarding Mama's condition was that everything she had placed any value on had been taken from her when the house burned. The mental meltdown was the result of that loss. They said she was clinically depressed and had had a nervous breakdown.

Daddy took us to see her as often as he could. I vaguely remember that she looked somehow diminished. Part of me believed that she got more than she bargained for because of her "breakdown." *Was it carefully orchestrated? Was it her attempt to have the attention focused on her?* These were questions that taunted me for many years. Somehow, I couldn't fathom that her life had been so tortuous as to come to this.

The woman I saw shuffling into the visiting room was not the woman who stood at home, feet planted firmly on the floor of her territory, defying anyone to take it away. This seemingly smaller woman smiled almost shyly, arms spread in greeting for a hug that felt foreign and uncomfortable. She declared in a voice dripping with what I viewed as feigned affection and in the third person, "Mama loves you, Mama misses y'all. Come see Mama." That woman wasn't the mother I knew. I didn't trust this person. I figured she wanted something I wouldn't want to give.

Daddy said Dr. Saint, Mama's psychiatrist, told him that she needed electric shock therapy treatments, which would help her forget the bad things that had happened. He said that it was a preferred treatment for catatonia. The electroconvulsive therapy was supposed to take away the painful memories of the fire, of losing her home, of Daddy's disabling illness and of the death of Maw Maw Linnie. *If this treatment would erase all of that, what else might it erase?* She would receive over one hundred of the treatments over the next year.

The time Mama was hospitalized passed all too quickly. For that duration, our home was quiet and peaceful. There had been no arguing or knockdown, drag-out fighting. Honestly, it felt as though we were on vacation or being allowed an opportunity to live in the make-believe world occupied by characters on television. Daddy cooked for us and we all sat down and ate together. Marbeth, Shirley, and a few neighbors cleaned the house for us. Neighbors checked on us and brought food. We were comfortable letting them in. And then Mama came home.

She was docile at first, fragile, needing care and attendance. Then the reality of her character slowly began reemerging. "What did Marbeth do with my towels? Where did y'all put my dishes? How did your daddy wash the clothes?" The answers to these questions seemed to provoke her wrath. She was very resentful that we had allowed others to "fool" with her things.

Those thoughts grew and grew until she was always in a foul mood. She accused all of us of having thrown or given away her stuff. No amount of explanation or evidence of some object she thought was missing could dissuade her from being resentful and belligerent.

The arguments began again. The older three of us began staying away from home as much as we could. It wasn't pleasant to spend the day with Mama. Janis and I would disappear for hours to play with Carmon and Christy, usually not even wanting to return home for dinner or supper. We came up with reasons to be invited to spend the night at their house.

For a while, Daddy or some family member had to chauffeur Mama to her appointments at the outpatient clinic at Central. Sometimes we were dropped at Aunt Claudie's or Maw Maw Lavinia's to wait for Mama's sessions or treatments to be over for the day. I hated going to either place, but especially to Aunt Claudie's house.

Mama's family handled her with kid gloves. We forever heard, "Poor Chrissie, poor Chrissie." They would shake their heads and lament over "everything that poor girl had been through." In the beginning, they were sympathetic toward Mama and Daddy; after all, he had been through a lot as well. They knew Pat O'Neal was a good man because at some point or another he had helped every one of them in some way. He was the one they called on when they had a legal or bureaucratic question or needed a letter written because of some personal jam.

They also knew he was devoted to his kids and to Mama. But they needed a scapegoat, someone to blame for what was happening to Chrissie. He drank, so it became convenient for them to pin the blame on him as being the reason Mama was sick. If Pat didn't drink, Chrissie would be "all right."

They were considerate of us for the most part early on. Mama's sisters made overtures about helping her with the house or with keeping us kids. They said she or Daddy could bring us to their homes anytime they needed to.

Oscar was always a country boy and was never comfortable "in town." He virtually became a permanent fixture at Frog and Marbeth's house. Since Oscar and Pogo were the same age, they were like brothers, inseparable. Oscar would arise at daybreak to go spend the day playing with Pogo. They stayed in the woods or built forts around the house.

Janis and I started staying with Maw Maw Lavinia. It made things simpler for Daddy for us just to stay over at her house whenever Mama had a doctor's appointment.

Jesse Patrick, as the youngest son, was still living with Maw Maw Lavinia then. He was fond of Janis and me, as were we of him. Often, he had our undivided attention as he shared tales of the mean nuns at parochial school. A conversation with Jesse revealed to me another mysterious aspect of religion. I was fascinated when he told me that a girl he knew had not swallowed the Host given to her by the priest at Holy Communion. Instead, she wrapped it up in a linen handkerchief and took it home. Jesse swore that when the girl opened the cloth in secret, that there was a spot of blood on the handkerchief. My thirteen-year-old eyes bugged at this story. I had never heard anything like that out in Ball. He would talk to us about subjects that none of Mama's other family members knew anything about.

Jesse Patrick was an enigmatic individual. Most often, he was light hearted, generous, and compassionate, but there was a dark quality about him as well. Once he reached adulthood, he seemed to have multiple ways of being. Shockingly, he married a much older woman, which created family talk. He was sometimes fiery when he got into one of his evangelical ravings about religion, for he had combined aspects of the Roman Catholic Church with fundamentalist dogmas into his own strange brand of faith.

At other times, he was a wine-drinking cockfighter who got down on his knees to blow life back into the bloody beak of a limp-necked rooster. Daddy spoke vaguely of Jesse Patrick's drag-queen forays into the nighttime world of gay clubs in Alexandria. He didn't live an openly gay lifestyle, but that didn't stop the family tongues from wagging about his adventures.

He loved popular music. Janis and I were crazy about the Beatles. We would have discussions and arguments with him about who was better, Elvis or the Beatles. I loved the Motown classic, "My Girl" by the Temptations; I credit Jesse Patrick with bringing it to my attention. I remember him running up the steps to my grandmother's house with that 45 in its paper jacket, waving it over his head, excitedly saying, "Y'all need to come listen to this new record I got!" He had been to Modern Record Shop in downtown Alexandria. We couldn't afford to go there often, but this storefront mecca, narrow in width but deep with bin after bin of the music we longed to get our hands on, housed all the Top 40 hits we salivated over and desired. Music, either on AM radio or 45s and LPs turning on a portable record player, was one of the balms Janis and I used to soothe away our worries and fears.

Another reason we didn't mind staying with Maw Maw Lavinia was that even for all her mean-spirited ways and stinginess we could at least sleep in a clean bedroom and bathe in a clean bathroom. She pretty much left us to our own devices after she got us to do housework or ironing. Her neglectfulness gave Janis and me opportunities to explore the surrounding neighborhoods or city streets near where she lived. I shudder to think now of how often we were alone, unsupervised, roaming areas we probably had no business in because our grandmother or one of our aunts simply let us go.

During the time I was in fifth grade, Mama's doctor visits became routine. Her obsessive need to collect also became routine. No amount of cajoling, lecturing, or begging could get her to stop. Any attempt to force her to stop was met with extreme episodes of cursing, threats, and manipulation. The hills of clothing and bags of stuff were now becoming mountains. The roaches Daddy had warned her about were now spotted routinely throughout our home. Mice also became a problem. The problem was magnified by the declarations of Mama's therapists who maintained that her depression was understandable due to her losses. Mama gained professional, sympathetic ears; this gave credence to her notion that her collecting was even more justifiable. Once she was able to drive herself to Central, it became almost ritualistic for her to treat herself to something new, either from a store or from Aunt Claudie's house.

Daddy tried to deal with the situation by maintaining levels of tolerance and patience, but even Job would have been worn out by the effort. Out of frustration and fear, he turned to Dr. Saint for help and advice as to how to handle Mama's obsessive need effectively. He described to the good doctor the way we were living.

Dr. Saint's response was, "Mr. O'Neal, your wife has had tremendous losses in her life, and therefore, what are a few roaches and rats in the house compared to happiness in the home?"

Daddy promptly let him know that he was crazy as hell before he abruptly left the doctor's office. It appeared that even the doctor was colluding with the disease. Daddy came home exasperated and drank to forget.

Chapter 10

The Irish Soul of My Father

Daddy's physical health steadily improved, but his emotional health remained fragile. He was never a person to sit idle for very long unless he was reading or watching something serious on television. Without something productive to do, he became exceedingly nervous. Daddy's hands shook uncontrollably. He spent unoccupied time pacing back and forth, as his tension or anxiety increased.

During the daytime, he worked in his large vegetable garden or in the yard. He was quite the horticulturist and had a variety of plants and shrubs in the yard that he regularly maintained. At one time, passersby might have considered our lush lawn a show place. The St. Augustine grass was so thick in some areas that our push mower would die out and have to be continually restarted.

Daddy's green thumb could make any plant thrive. I recall how he explained to me the way to graft one plant to another. I watched him make small notches with his pocketknife into the tender green branches of one azalea and then diagonally cut another branch from a different bush. Once this was done, he would insert the severed limb into the notch of the first branch. He'd wrap that area carefully with garden tape or plastic and then just as carefully watch it until the attached branch rooted. He loved those dwarf azaleas. He had successfully grafted a pink-blossomed branch onto a red-blossomed bush. It was amazing to see a single bush with two different-colored blooms!

Over the years, Mama's illness took its toll on his enthusiasm for keeping up the yard. He often said he felt hypocritical for maintaining a nice yard while the house was becoming a junk pile. His interest waned to the point that he only kept the grounds mowed. As we kids got older, it became our responsibility to help him with that chore.

He did keep his vegetable garden. He planted green onions, cabbage, tomatoes, and peppers. The years of new potatoes, green beans, cucumbers, corn, and other vegetables were a wonderful part of my childhood, but Daddy lost interest in having a sizeable garden as Mama's disorder gained steam. Mama never fully appreciated or utilized the abundance he could produce. She didn't see it as a remarkable gift, as something Daddy had mastered by steadily working and honing his skill. The food would go unused unless Daddy sold it or gave it away, which became his custom.

Once, when I was young, I went with him to a house way down a dirt road and far back in the woods up in rural Grant Parish. Daddy was going to take a bushel of potatoes to a family. A cloud of dust followed the pickup as we made our way down the bumpy, rutted road. Dogs bayed a greeting as Daddy parked parallel to their front porch.

Daddy slid out from underneath the steering wheel of his old pickup as the man of the house came out to greet him. As he waited beside the open truck door, Daddy took the ever-present red or blue bandana out of his overall pocket to wipe away the sweat that had gathered on his forehead under the brim of his straw hat. He and the man exchanged greetings and walked to the front of the truck to talk. Each of them hitched up one of their pants legs to prop a work-boot-shod foot onto the front bumper.

I was a little apprehensive about getting out of the truck—I didn't know the people. I gazed around the property and wondered why they lived so far in the woods. About that time, two droopy, mangy-looking hound dogs loped around the corner of the house. Their movements made me notice something in the shadows of the porch.

The low-hanging porch roof cast a deep shadow and the brightness of the midmorning sun made it hard to distinguish what was on the porch. I had to squint hard to focus. Suddenly, I realized there was a girl sitting on a ladder-back chair. She methodically rocked her upper body back and forth. She held her head tilted severely to the right, as if she were gazing at something up high. It occurred to me that I shouldn't be staring at her; maybe she was embarrassed. I decided to continue reading the library book I had brought along in the truck.

Daddy came around to the truck door and told me I could get out if I wanted to. I decided to stretch my legs. I made my way around the truck, which brought me closer to the porch. I couldn't help looking in the girl's direction. She wasn't much older than I was, but her body was thin and pale, which gave me the impression that she seemed like a helpless baby or an old woman. She held her stick-thin arms close against her body so that her forearms lay on her thighs, palms up. The most frightening aspect of seeing her up close was that her mouth hung open and spit drooled down her chin as hundreds of black houseflies swarmed around her head. I quickly got back into the truck.

Daddy gave the bushel of potatoes to the man and we left. My curiosity and concern were gnawing a hole in me. I had to wait to ask Daddy about the girl until we were on the smooth highway so that I could be heard above the roar of the truck straining out of the woods.

I asked, "Daddy, what was wrong with that girl?"

He replied, "She's retarded, baby, she can't help the way she is."

I asked many "but why" questions and Daddy patiently answered each one.

He informed me that she was about twelve years old, that she had to wear a diaper, and that her family had to feed her. Finally, I asked whether her family would always have to take care of her. Daddy told me that they could have placed her in Pinecrest State School, which was located five miles south of our home, in Kingsville. In those days, the place was known as the Colony, where developmentally disabled individuals were housed.

Daddy said he doubted that would ever happen because the people were too proud. He said they took care of the girl the best they knew how, but that they were just ignorant, poor people who didn't know better. He said he tried to stop by every now and then to see about them and to bring vegetables, squirrels, or fish. Daddy said the old boy was a hard worker but stayed laid off most of the time and they had many mouths to feed.

One of the greatest pleasures my father derived from life was to give to others. He garnered great joy from being able to do so.

Daddy stayed close to home as his recuperation continued. As Mama's demands and tantrums grew worse, and once she was able to get out again, he didn't see the need to babysit her all the time. More than likely, like his children, he couldn't tolerate being stuck with her all day. He began going fishing and hunting more, depending on the season. Just as we did, he found ways not to have to be at home.

Daddy knew the countryside as well as his brother Wig. They had hunted and fished all over Rapides and Grant parishes. Daddy would make the circuit—up to Larto Lake above Colfax, Louisiana, out to Saline Lake, in the eastern portion of Rapides Parish, and back up to the Little River and Hard Water Lake north of our house in Grant Parish. He never owned one of the big, expensive bass rigs like some other guys in the "Sportsman's Paradise." Daddy preferred a little, fourteen-foot aluminum boat that he could readily pull on a trailer behind his pickup.

Often, as he made his rounds to see where the fish were biting, Daddy would stop and talk to the locals to get feedback. He told a story about encountering a young black boy fishing on a bayou near Colfax. As Daddy slowly drove along the "by," as we say in Louisiana, he saw that the boy had a stringer full of big bream hanging from a nearby tree. Daddy parked his pickup and walked over to see what kind of bait the boy was using to catch such a nice mess of fish.

The boy was no more than twelve years old. He indicated to Daddy that he was using some "big ol' night crawlers, but you know they keep bitin' me."

Daddy looked into the bait bucket and realized the boy had been using baby ground rattlers mixed in with the night crawlers. He told the boy to stop and get himself home as quick as he could and to be sure to tell his mama that he'd been fishing with snakes. Every time he told the story, he grinned and shook his head, saying, "That beat all I had ever seen!"

Daddy knew the sweet spots for bream or white perch. He showed my first husband, Johnny, and my son, Patrick, many choice spots to hunt or fish. My cousin Dennis, Aunt Jettie's son, still speaks fondly of how "Uncle Pat" was the only real father figure he knew as a child. He was appreciative of the times Daddy spent with him. Daddy made a deliberate effort to include Dennis and my other male relatives on trips to the woods, rivers, or bayous to experience life in the outdoors.

When Daddy talked about the outdoors, there was a sense of reverence, respect, and wonder in his words about what he believed a higher power had created. He was a conservationist who challenged political leaders and his peers to do right by the environment and the creatures of the wild. He abhorred waste and thought that anyone who overcaught or overkilled was out of line. When he got older, he told me that he still liked to go hunting but thought he would rather have been able to paint or photograph what he saw in the woods as a way to record it as opposed to taking a gun.

A favorite place of his to take us on a summer outing was to White Sulphur Springs in LaSalle Parish off Louisiana 8. Once, Daddy bought an old school bus some errant hippie had painted psychedelic purple. It was a little embarrassing to Janis and me to ride down the highway in that "can't miss" bus, but we did have a few good times out on the creek bank. My father and those relatives who might have joined us would barbeque on our Old Smokey while we kids played in the cold creek water. We'd bring watermelons and place them in the water in the shade of an overhanging tree branch.

Before the day was out, Daddy would instruct us to go to the natural spring that smelled to high heaven of rotten eggs. There, we would bathe any summer sores we might have in the flowing water. Someone had connected a pipe with a spigot to the spring, making it convenient to collect the water in jugs or to wash in the icy water. The high sulphur content of the water gave it the noxious smell—but it never lingered on the skin. Boils, or what we called "risings," cleared up a few days after bathing in the water.

A quick summer thunderstorm sent us all running for the bus one time. Daddy hurriedly put the aluminum Old Smokey in the back of the bus. We headed back home with that little pit cooking away—smoke boiling out the back window of the bus.

When we quit using the bus, Daddy parked it on the side of the house as a place to raise rabbits. That didn't last too long because Mama crowded the rabbits out with one of her collections of furniture and household goods. It was a good place to sneak stuff away.

Daddy always looked for some project in order to make a little money. He was hard-pressed to support his family on disability benefits alone. Sometimes he'd buy a load of something, like watermelons, at a bargain price. He would have the back of his pickup loaded to the top of the bed when he brought them home for us to sell in front of the house. We spent many summer days with a wooden pallet full of cantaloupes or watermelons in front of the house; a makeshift sign advertised them as two for a dollar or four for a dollar as the season waned. He did this so we could learn the value of a dollar and perhaps earn enough spending money to last through summer vacation.

My father's brain was perpetually in drive, figuring out a way to make things a little better for us financially. Sometimes he sold some of the vegetables he raised; sometimes it was rabbits, red worms, or catalpa worms. A large, wooden box set up off the ground with a wood-framed, screened lid was where he kept the red worms. Daddy moistened layers of the newspaper he read daily and then placed them on top of the worms. It was fascinating to see how they burrowed through that newspaper in a relatively short time. We didn't realize then that these simple, humble acts performed by Daddy showed us the value of repurposing what others saw as garbage. We often watched as he lifted a handful of the wriggling creatures into buckets for the fishermen who stopped to buy them as fish bait.

In Daddy's later years, he deliberately set about turning the backyard into an orchard of catalpa trees. The fast-growing southern catalpa, with its large, vivid green leaves and sweet-smelling white blossoms were home to the larvae of the catalpa sphinx moth. Those "catalpa worms" were excellent fish bait. Daddy or Oscar would harvest the worms, tromping through the green droppings before the worms completely defoliated the trees.

Before the town of Ball had sanitation service, folks used fifty-gallon metal drums to burn their trash or used them to place garbage in for independent hauler pick-up service. Daddy turned that into a sideline business. He drove all over several parishes to various oil companies to purchase the barrels. Once he got them home, he cut the lids out of one end and then placed them at the end of his drive with a homemade sign selling them for fifteen dollars a barrel.

To supplement his Social Security, he began to work a little. Ever mindful of Mama and her sister's meanness toward each other, he never worked more than was allowed according to the rules of receiving disability. In a mad fit, one of them could very easily report him to the Social Security administration and risk his monthly benefits out of nothing more than spite.

Daddy became involved with some house movers and acted as a sort of straw boss on some of their jobs. He came home with tales of moving houses and the difficulties of dealing with local law enforcement, zoning laws, old hauling rigs, used equipment, and young men willing to risk their necks to make a few bucks. He loved the adventure of this kind of work. It kept him functioning in the working man's world.

Daddy liked problem solving and figuring out ways to do difficult things. He jokingly told me that he would love to help move one of the largest buildings in downtown Alexandria—a ten-story bank building. He believed it could have been done!

A story he loved to tell was about the time they had to move a house and set it down on a concrete slab. The problem came from the fact that they couldn't place the house on a pier-and-beam system because the owner wanted it flush with the slab. The crew Daddy worked with decided to set the house down on fifty-pound blocks of ice placed strategically over the surface of the concrete to act as temporary piers.

Another problem arose when the ice started melting faster on the sunny side of the house. That situation might have caused the house to tilt dangerously. Daddy came up with the solution. He told one of the crewmen to use a water hose to spray the shaded ice so that it would melt at approximately the same pace as the other side. It worked. The house settled into place without the use of an expensive, hard-to-place set of jacks and pulleys.

On hot summer evenings when Daddy came home, his wiry body absolutely dripped sweat. His hands violently shook and the skin around his eyes was pale and sunken.

His legs often cramped up on him because he would lose so much fluid in a day's time. He'd sit with his shirt off, drink water, and take salt tablets while he cooled off.

No matter what might take him away during the day, he made a point of being home by the time we got in from school. Within thirty to forty-five minutes after any one of us came in from school on any given day, someone inevitably ended up in a shouting match with Mama. The only way to avoid confrontations was to quickly fix a snack of some kind and get the hell out of the house. Knowing Daddy would be home before too long became a stabilizing source of comfort to us. I believe he felt that he had to be home to referee the evening's events. He could keep Mama off our backs and squelch any possible attempts on her part to abuse us physically.

When Daddy was sober, he was a quiet, thoughtful man who seemed to absorb the world's problems like a sponge. Once that sponge-like mind of his saturated itself with the issues that concerned or affected him, his release was to drink.

For many years, I was in denial about his alcoholism. *He only drinks beer*, I thought, *he isn't mean and nasty, and he loves us*. But his drinking worried me. The hellacious arguments between Mama and Daddy most often occurred when he had been drinking. This was when he could face down Mama, when he had the courage to rail against her hard-nosed intolerance of him and us children.

Daddy didn't like conflict or confrontation whether he was drinking or not. Even corporal punishment, a tried-and-true Southern tradition (and Mama's preferred method of discipline), pained him terribly. He said a switching when we were little might be necessary, but when we reached the age of reason, "a good talking-to" should do the trick. And it did, coming from him.

It bothered us kids if Daddy was disappointed in something we might have done. We felt palpable shame in even the most minor infractions because we didn't want to see his hurt reaction. Daddy's Irish soul was both a blessing and a curse; tears came easily to the man who loved so much, especially if he saw one of his children hurt. He shared his mama's belief that "when your children are little they step on your feet, and when they're older they step on your heart." We knew that we were cherished by Daddy and that our well-being was his chief concern.

As Mama's illness became less tolerable, he drank to hide the pain and frustration of not knowing what to do. In his estimation, she was sick; to be harsh to someone who was crippled went against everything he believed in. Daddy's compassion was overwhelming. So when family or close friends would ask, "Why don't you put your foot down with Christine and make her clean up that house?" it was not an easy question for him to answer. For him, that action was much easier said than done. How was he supposed to put his foot down?

He considered himself not only Mama's husband, but her protector as well. His belief system and traditional values said he must look after her, provide for her, and protect her to the best of his abilities. Many, many times he told me he had made a vow to God to look after Mama. His passive-aggressive stance took root just as slowly as Mama's obsessive-compulsive hoarding.

Even in a tortured household, not every minute is filled with bad things. The interludes between can be calm and hopeful. People have a chance to catch their breath, to laugh for a few moments, or to feel good about the days ahead. Therefore, quietly, the dark tentacles grow and snake themselves in and out, in and out, until all the living, breathing beings are entangled and don't know how to find a way out. That's the way it was for my family.

Many of Daddy's sober moments were spent in study and contemplation. He was a genius, a member of Mensa. Not many knew the significance of that association. But everyone in his family considered him a smart man. They said there wasn't much he couldn't do or that he couldn't figure out. Many of them were amazed that he came up with ways to make money out of nothing.

Late evenings would find him reading the paper or watching the nightly news. He paid close attention to world events and to local politics. Daddy had an enormous love and respect for the United States and our way of life, but he was troubled by injustices, prejudices toward the downtrodden, and the plight of the working poor. Firing off a letter to the editor of the *Town Talk* to express his views was something Daddy didn't give a second thought to. Over the years, he authored numerous letters that were published. Readers came to know the name Patrick O'Neal in the late '70s and all through the '80s for submitting commentaries about local and national politics and social issues.

In 1987 Daddy sent one of his published "letters to the editor" clipped from the newspaper to the governor, Edwin Edwards. The embattled, controversial governor responded in a letter dated August 17, 1987. In it, Edwards said Daddy's opinion (that the continual criticism of Edwards's administration would not resolve their problems) "is one that everyone in the state should consider." Daddy beamed at having gotten the governor to take notice of his thoughts.

Daddy was a deep thinker and a prolific reader. Writing seemed to be a necessary outlet for him to maintain his sanity. I kept many of his notebooks that were filled with his thoughts on a variety of subjects. I often wondered how difficult it must have been for him to exist in a world surrounded by folks who couldn't comprehend the depths of his thoughts. He never indicated that he felt that way, as he considered himself a common, working-class man, superior to no one. But as his daughter, I could hear a need in his voice, a need to engage with someone who could grasp the subject matter, someone who could verbally joust with him and hold his own. Many people thought his commentaries were just ramblings, but many others also knew that the things he talked about were way over their heads. To this day, I'll occasionally run into someone who still remembers something Daddy said or wrote.

I was often the one he shared his thoughts with, the one he could converse with, the one who had the capacity to understand the seriousness of the subjects he wanted to discuss. This helped make me the enemy in Mama's eyes. Daddy and I shared a world she could never enter. It wasn't that we intentionally left her out; she wasn't interested, nor did she understand. We unwittingly set up a dynamic that further fueled Mama's resentment. Her resentment and need to control the household gave her ammunition to blast away when he drank.

I remember only once feeling sympathetic toward Mama during a fight. The fight was loud and frightening to us kids. I remember watching from across the room, fearful that somebody was going to get hurt. I was nine years old, but I thought and hoped that I could get them to calm down.

I approached Mama. She stood defiantly, hefty shoulders and chest lunging forward as Daddy angrily filibustered about the way her hoarding was affecting the household. I'm not sure why I was drawn to her defense. Maybe it was because I had begged Daddy to stop talking. His steady stream of frustrated ranting was making me anxious. He was on a venting roll and he wouldn't stop.

As I reached to hug Mama, pleading with her just not to argue with him, I remember the look on her face. Not once did her eyes meet mine. She was so focused on Daddy, I was nothing more than a buzzing fly, annoying her with its presence. Her lips were tightly pinched, the corners of them drawn harshly down. Her forehead was wrinkled, and her eyes . . . her eyes shot laser darts Daddy's way.

Vainly I tried to capture her attention. Crying and begging I pleaded, "Mama, please stop fighting!" She continued to ignore me so I reached up to embrace her around the neck. "Mama, Mama, I love you."

With a force I will never forget, she shoved my reaching arms away and said, "Frances Evelyn, get out of here!" And so I did. I never expressed that sincere emotion to her again.

Their fights continued, some were awful, some were just sad to listen to from my perspective. To avoid them, Daddy would leave, sometimes overnight. I think he believed that if he weren't present, she would calm down. Usually that was the case, but more often than not, she went into high gear to find out where he was and to see if he was spending money. When he scattered, we usually did too.

Those nights were tense. Often Mama would have demanded that we look up the number to the package liquor store he frequented. It was embarrassing to hear her call the place to see if he was there. Sometimes she ranted on about how someone was going to knock him in the head for his money to whoever answered the phone. Most often, she just ranted at us. We went to bed listening to her screaming that we would find him dead in a ditch somewhere the next day.

I spent many of those nights lying awake, listening for him to open the front door, but knowing that after nine o'clock, he wouldn't be coming home. He never, ever drove when he drank. I put the pillow over my head and cried and prayed that God would keep him safe and bring him back home.

Sometimes Mama went looking for him. She got Shirley to drive her to town. Sometimes she would have Shirley go into the beer joint to get him. Sometimes she just drove his truck home. Eventually, Daddy would call her to pick him up.

If one or all of us kids were around, then she might make us go with her. It was humiliating to be forced to go inside to get him. Her shrewish behavior was well known by Daddy's acquaintances. They would make snide catcalls and other obnoxious remarks when they saw one of us kids coming in to get Daddy. "Better go on, Pat, Mama's gonna be pissed off and whip your ass."

Most of the time Daddy would good-naturedly take their ribbing; he'd talk a few minutes longer and then leave. It was rare that he let their comments annoy him, but occasionally he would tell us to "get back to the car, tell your mama I'll be there when I get good and goddamned ready."

I suppose I could have resented him for staying away. If I did, it didn't last long. I sympathized with him. I wanted to leave too. I came to understand that Daddy was tolerant to a fault, but when his tolerance waned, so did his patience. Sober, he could never fully confront Mama. Drinking loosened his normal reserve. Even so, he couldn't give as well as he got. It was impossible to reason with Mama whether he was drunk or sober. It wasn't characteristic of him to be hateful to her, so for the most part, she got her way like a willful child.

She demanded his time, his consideration, his money, his soul. He was hers—nobody else could have him. In order to get some respite from her tirades, he sought out conversation with anybody who would listen. Instead of complaining or whining about how she was, Daddy used conversations about politics and social issues and Old Milwaukee beer as his way to release his pent-up anger and frustration with Mama.

Once, when I was a teenager, Daddy and Mama had a particularly bad fight—again, over the subject of letting us clean up the house. When she refused, he told her he was leaving and taking us with him. And we did. We spent the night in a small motel in Alexandria. The next morning Daddy and I talked about what we were going to do. I begged him to get us another place to live. To my way of thinking, we could just leave Mama at home and never go back. Daddy seemed to consider it for a brief time.

Soon he shook his head, and with his wry, crooked smile, he said, "I'm sorry, baby, but it won't work."

I couldn't understand why that wasn't a good plan. He explained to me that Mama had no source of income and that none of her family would be willing to take her into their homes. Daddy believed that the judicial system would not allow him to have complete custody of us—more than likely, she would have been given custodial rights. He was afraid that if the authorities came into our home and saw the conditions we lived in, then we would be taken away.

Daddy also considered that even if he established a decent home for us that Mama's sisters or mother would have made trouble for him. That was the first time I ever felt impotent. We were backed against a wall. The only thing left to do was to go back home.

No matter how bad things might get or how low on funds we sometimes were, we could count on Daddy to come through in times of need or to satisfy one of our childish wishes.

Almost every summer we would whine or complain about wanting a swimming pool. For several years, Daddy bought us the largest plastic swimming pool he could afford. Those pools never lasted longer than one season. It seemed ridiculous to him to continue wasting money on something that wouldn't hold up.

His solution was to buy the largest galvanized cow tank he could find. It measured about twelve feet in circumference but was only about three feet deep. Daddy attached a spigot so that when we needed to drain and clean the pool, we simply turned the valve on the spigot and the water slowly drained. When the water level got below the spigot line, we had to bail with plastic buckets to get the rest of the water out. I can still hear the thunderous sound of that galvanized metal tank as we lifted it. We learned quickly that if we wanted to have fun in it, we would have to join to lift it on one side to finish draining it. As a team, my sisters and brother, Carmon and Christy, and I would continue bailing water or clean the inside with Comet before setting it back down and then filling it with the water hose.

We created quite a stir with that "pool." People passing on Ball Cut-Off Road would slow down to see what we were doing. Sometimes Daddy would sit under the sweet gum trees, watching us cutting up in the pool, going round and round to make a "current" that would propel us dizzyingly in circles if we stopped. Daddy would laugh at us and then holler, "How ya'll, and ya Mama and them?" at passing motorists, which would tickle us and embarrass us all at the same time.

I didn't join many school organizations, partly because it might have cost money to be involved. I knew we couldn't afford it. By the time I reached high school, choir seemed a safe elective, so I became part of the junior mixed chorus. Near the end of my sophomore year, I was confronted with having to get a dress for the spring concert. I told Mama that I would need to get one, but she didn't seem concerned. When I told Daddy, he said he wasn't sure if we could spare the money—it was the middle of the month, but he would see what he could do.

I stressed for days about having to go to that concert without anything decent to wear. A few days before the concert, Daddy came in one evening and quietly slipped me thirty dollars.

"You think you can get what you need with that?" he asked. I hid my amazement and excitement about that amount of money—it seemed like a fortune.

I got Christy Thibodeaux to drive me to town to look for a dress. I bought a sweet, pale-pink cotton voile dress that had long sleeves that ended in soft ruffles at the wrist. I even had enough left to buy a pair of light-pink leather Mary Janes. Every time I looked at the tiny, dark-pink rosebuds printed on the dotted Swiss fabric, I felt a special thrill.

After the concert, Mama diminished my thrill over the dress when she let me know that Daddy had hocked his shotgun in order to give me the money for the dress. It seemed as though she took spiteful satisfaction in sharing that information.

I know that Daddy spent too much time worrying over not having enough money to buy the things he thought we were missing out on, the things that our peers were able to have. When times were good, he tried his best to make our lives more enjoyable. We knew when he had a little extra money in his pockets because he would trade his denim overalls, work boots, and his ever-present pipe for a pair of khakis, button-up dress shirt, brown wing tips, and a cigar. If he came into the house with a glint in his eyes and the sweet smell of cigar smoke trailing behind, we knew we were in for a treat.

My daddy, my papa-daddy . . . the person who taught me so much; I miss him still. He deserved so much more from life than he got.

Chapter 11

No Place Like Home

I was in fifth grade when Mama started sinking deeper into her obsessive world. She also seemed to get meaner as the days passed. When you're ten or eleven, you don't understand why just "being" seems to bother someone so much. We were disturbances to her day. She didn't want to have to attend to our childish needs. For the most part, we fended for ourselves.

I wouldn't intellectually understand until much, much later that from her point of view, we had to be watched, not for the sake of our safety, but because we daily upset her perception of control. When we were near, when we touched her things, her sense of control shifted. Essentially, as the old childhood rhyme said, we were stepping on the crack that would break her back—something bad *might* happen or *would* happen if we "messed" with her things.

The medications the psychiatrist prescribed for Mama were the old '60s antidepressants like Elavil, and they made her lethargic and lazy. She occupied the majority of her time sitting, talking on the phone, or watching the soap operas, which she viewed as some type of weird reality.

Daddy came in one evening to find her on the phone talking about someone suffering a terrible illness. Mama was discussing the latest catastrophe she saw on *Days of Our Lives*. Catching only the tail end of the horrible tragedy, Daddy said his heart was in his throat. He attempted to signal Mama to have her explain what was going on, believing some family member was hurt or in dire straits. She waved him off until she finished her conversation.

Afterward, she proceeded to fill him in, just as if in fact she had been speaking about a family member.

Finally, Daddy said, "Christine, who in God's name are you talking about?"

She vehemently chastised him by replying, "Oh hell, you know! Julie and Doug on TV!"

Daddy rolled his eyes, shook his head, and resigned himself that her soap-opera obsession was annoying but harmless. She never put that much energy into being concerned about real people, though.

Mama performed only the essential chores around the house, like washing dishes or clothes and preparing an evening meal. As Janis and I got older, we wanted to help, but Mama wouldn't let us "mess and gum" as she referred to our attempts to learn to cook or be in the kitchen. She considered that we didn't wash the dishes "right," we didn't "rench" them clean enough. Every attempt we made to clean up was met with some kind of resistance or her standard insistence that she would "take care of it later." It felt wrong to be resentful of Mama because she wouldn't let us do chores around the house. Our friends' complaints about being overworked at home by their parents fell on deaf ears—oh, to have that problem!

Janis, Kitty, and I all became very adept at cleaning houses for other people because we watched the way Mama scrubbed, when she did clean. This was evidence of her perfectionist nature; we just didn't know it at the time. My sisters and I were severely influenced by this trait. We definitely understood the irony involved when other people wanted us to help them clean house but our own mother would bitch and raise hell if we wanted to do the same thing at home.

Most often, we prepared our own breakfast and dinner (lunch). Sometimes, Mama cooked a big pot of oatmeal for breakfast, but it would sit on the stove for the rest of the day. Daddy, Oscar, and I were early risers. We liked oatmeal and usually made toast to go along with it. We used the broiler in the oven to make the toast. Although we had various toasters over the years, we rarely used them because we couldn't find them under the piles of bread wrappers, paper bags, plastic bowls, glasses, dishes, pots, and pans, a hoarder's paraphernalia, which hid them from view. These items took up every inch of space on the countertop. The stove and oven were far more assessable at that time because Mama had to have them to prepare our meager meals.

Our meals consisted of foods that Mama would boil or stew. She wouldn't let her creativity emerge in meal preparation. Money was tight; I don't recall ever having much red meat with the exception of hamburger. Mama cooked simple Southern foods like cabbage, mustard greens, beans and rice, boiled potatoes, liver, and her infamous stews. None of these meals required a tremendous amount of effort to prepare.

She purchased beef stew meat that was mostly fat. She stewed the meat down with hunks of red potatoes, whole canned tomatoes, and onions in a large pot. It wasn't particularly bad nor was it particularly good, but at least she put some effort into this occasional meal. Mama did excel at cooking red pinto beans, which she left for hours unattended.

She cooked a large pot of white rice to go with them. After years of practice using Maw Maw Linnie's recipe, she turned out delicious pones of cornbread to go with the beans and rice. Mama had no love for the art of cooking; she chose what was easiest for her to offer. Her cooking netted huge quantities of food, which might stay as leftovers in the ice box (as we called it) for days.

Daddy made sure we were never out of milk, peanut butter, and eggs. With those things, he knew we would have something to eat if Mama shut down and wouldn't cook. Daddy actually loved to cook, but if he went into the kitchen to do so, he would bring to bear Mama's wrath. On those rare occasions, when he was prepared to endure Mama's nagging, ironically, over him making a mess, we could look forward to something other than Mama's boring food.

The times we ate special things were when Daddy cooked. With a bit of flair, he whipped up batter to make flapjacks and french toast for us; sometimes he prepared his own simple syrup to go with those treats.

Most often, he stuck to dishes he could prepare outdoors, such as barbecued chicken, the occasional armadillo or goat, and fried bream, catfish, and alligator.

At holidays, he prepared cornbread dressing and fruit salad using ingredients Mama didn't ordinarily use, such as celery, bell peppers, coconuts, and pineapple. She loudly complained about his mess, but he ignored it because he liked those special times of the year. We all shook our heads and laughed or made sarcastic remarks about her ridiculous complaints.

When any of us disrupted Mama's regular routine, she was most uncomfortable, caught off-guard, and agitated. The way she expressed that discomfort was to nag, cajole, or scream at us until we gave up and left so as not to hear her.

Holidays and special events made her particularly nervous. If she thought that any one of us wanted to touch or rearrange any of her things in preparation of a holiday, then her agitation intensified. Once she put something somewhere, that's where she intended for it to stay forever. She always knew if we touched something too. And the thought of anyone from outside the immediate family coming anywhere near our house sent her into high anxiety. Mama would start rattling off excuses as to why she didn't want anyone around.

Being the avid outdoorsman that he was, Daddy (and Oscar as he got older) provided us with a lot of game meat. Mama didn't complain about cooking the squirrels or rabbits he brought home because they were free, but we girls weren't always thrilled about them. Daddy said squirrel brains made him smart!

I remember many fall and winter evenings checking the pots on the stove to find tiny squirrel limbs cooked down in a pot of rice (like jambalaya), with a pot of mustard greens, cornbread in a black-iron skillet, and baked sweet potatoes as sides. It was simple fare; one benefit of it was that none of us kids suffered from high cholesterol.

Grocery shopping was one area where Mama's obsessive-compulsive tendencies were quite evident. She bought in large quantities and usually shopped for dented, off-brands to save money and to get more for her buck. When Daddy's Social Security check came in at the beginning of the month, she bought food for the rest of the month. She wouldn't buy cereal she thought we might like and therefore eat quickly. There were usually several boxes of plain Kellogg's cornflakes scattered around the kitchen. The only one of us who grew to like them was Oscar, who, though small, could eat a huge bowlful. They would definitely last the entire month because nobody ate them! And she never threw the boxes away. Only Oscar knew which box had the freshest cereal and the least amount of roaches crawling in it.

Mama also bought the cheapest, largest jar of peanut butter imaginable. The only way to eat the dry glob was to add jelly or syrup to it to thin it down so it could be more easily spread on the loaves and loaves of white bread Mama bought. Eventually, we just put the peanut butter into a cup or bowl, poured enough syrup on it to make it creamy, and crumbled the day-old bread she bought into the mix so that it was palatable. I told my siblings that it was goulash.

When Mama shopped, she made sure the baggers at the grocery store put the food in cardboard boxes. That's usually where they stayed throughout the month. She placed the boxes on the floor of the kitchen or under the table leaving only a narrow pathway to walk. We never put the groceries away in cabinets because the cabinets never got used. Besides, Mama couldn't see her stuff if they got stored away. The cabinets were purposed for hiding, not for daily use. Years later, we might find various cans of food like pork and beans that she had squirreled away in the cabinets we never opened.

We didn't know what it was like to sit at a dining table and eat a meal as a family on a regular basis, unless Mama wasn't home. That vital part of a functioning family was something we kids craved as a way of feeling normal.

We had a Formica table in the kitchen; we just never saw it. There might have been one or two chairs positioned at the table, but they were unusable as well. Mama used these surfaces for stacking items. It wasn't unusual to have a large, plastic snowman or "walk-with-me" doll occupying one of the chairs. The doll or snowman was perched atop various piles of newspapers, folded sheets or towels, plastic flowers, and assorted bagged items sitting on or hanging from the chair, which then elevated the items above the tabletop.

Mama used the kitchen table for everything except the purpose for which it was intended. The top of the table was the resting place for all sorts of things: vases, dishes, mail, cooking utensils, various pots and pans, aluminum boilers, or cast-iron Dutch ovens used to fry fish, which would still have the hardened shortening in them. Roaches, mosquito hawks, and spiders were captured in the solidified, putrid lard.

The far corner of the kitchen cabinet next to the outside wall was a sort of no-man's land. Years might go by before anyone got close to that forbidden zone. Mama used that space between the counter and table to stack boxes and bags. There might be boxes of canning jars that contained pickles, figs, pears, jelly, and homemade preserves. The rare times when the space got cleared, the unfortunate one who undertook the task might have been surprised by the collapsing of a sodden box. A chemical reaction of built-up gases produced when the preserved food got too hot would sometimes cause them to burst spontaneously. It wasn't pleasant to find yourself bent over with the wilted sides in your hands staring at a mess of broken glass, gray pickles, and the vinegary remnant of cardboard stuck to the linoleum. There's nothing like opening a jar of preserved pickles that has been sitting in the heat for four or five years. The rancid vinegar smell could revive a dead horse!

Essentially, the only floor surfaces available to walk were the spots in front of the sink, the stove, the refrigerator, and the narrow walkway from the back door leading to the living room. Every inch of the floor was covered by something. Next to the stove and to the right of the interior door was a small folding table where Mama placed various items that sat dangerously above and underneath the table. Sometimes these things were scorched by their exposure to our main heat source.

As these things increased in number, there was no way to keep the house clean. Crumbs of food, roach shit, mice droppings, dust, mold, and mildew all mixed together and kept shifting in and out, depending on what was placed on top of the heap. Had an archeologist dug through the layers, years of what might have been going on in our household would have been revealed.

The kitchen wasn't very big, maybe ten by fourteen feet, so there wasn't much room to play with. The corners of the kitchen ceiling usually had enormous cobwebs hanging down. Spiders would attach their long silvery threads to the paper bags on the floor and then onto the plastic curtains hanging in the windows. Although it had an eastern exposure, there wasn't much light in the kitchen because too many things blocked the sun.

Sometimes, after reading a book that inspired me about how other people lived, I would fantasize about what it might feel like to rip those ugly, floral plastic curtains away, exposing glass I could clean of its grime. I imagined light sparkling off silverware and china on a white linen tablecloth. I could picture a room filled with sunlight where the shadows played off pristine surfaces.

The ancient refrigerator was small and rounded at the top; its handle was vertical and difficult to manipulate. We had to jerk it down to open the door, which made the whole thing shake and rattle. We had to learn how to get it opened with the least amount of noise possible or we got hollered at for "messin'" with stuff. Depending on the force used, you either knocked something off the top or out of the refrigerator, which would guarantee a good "ass chewing" from Mama.

For many years the milk company, Foremost, delivered milk to homes in our area. Daddy got the service for our family. Kitty remembers getting a bad beating from Mama for causing a glass gallon jug of that milk to fall on the linoleum floor. Whole milk and shards of glass flew everywhere. Immediately, the milk soaked the paper bags and boxes lining the path through the kitchen. Now, Mama would be compelled to mop the floor and wash the contents of the bags of clothes that acted as sentries and buffers of her worldview.

Kitty ran from the house as fast as she could to get away from Mama. Mama knew she couldn't catch her, so she insisted that Janis retrieve her and bring her back to the house. My little sister tried to hide in a deep, deep ditch next to the railroad tracks less than a quarter mile from home.

Janis found her though and dragged her back to Mama for her punishment. The lapse in time didn't cool Mama down—she furiously beat Kitty with a belt. The idea of understanding that a child could be clumsy and incapable of handling such a load was inconceivable to Mama. She was annoyed and angry, not only because of the wasted milk, but also because she would have to clean up the mess. Kitty had to suffer the consequences for Mama's inconvenience.

Opening the door of the refrigerator revealed a nightmare inside! Most of the time, the appliance light was burned out. We had to delve in the dark to find something edible. That refrigerator matured us; we learned how to cut off the moldy parts of cheese and then melt it on bread in the toaster-oven to make it more palatable. The majority of the food kept getting pushed back so we had no idea what was in there or how long it had been in there. Our noses became adept at ferreting out what was edible and what wasn't.

Mama bought inexpensive blocks of margarine wrapped in thin, waxed, tissue-like paper. It absorbed every smell in the refrigerator, which made it absolutely awful tasting. Heating it up did nothing to change the taste or the aroma. Most of us eventually came to use the refrigerator only to get milk or water from the communal jug unless we knew exactly how long some item had been in there.

Although Mama ran by no particular schedule, except for gossipy phone calls or designated soap opera times, she had our evening meals finished by four o'clock. As we came in from school or Daddy from wherever he might have been, we ate separately. Usually, this was in front of the TV. It would have been exceedingly difficult for us to eat together as a family in those claustrophobic surroundings.

Mama made a concerted effort to keep a space clear on the couch for Daddy to sit; otherwise, she might have had to endure his rare anger when his patience grew thin over the ever-expanding gathering of goods. It was as if they were locked into a weird chess game. It played out between them perpetually. Mama knew just how much Daddy would take before he blew. She would sneak things in during the day if he went somewhere.

Her way of compromising was to not place things within his immediate view, which might remind him of her actions. Like many men, he didn't see new things right away, especially if she hid them. The mountains just continued to rise slowly.

After a fashion, we simply had to turn away from her acquisitions because the price we had to pay for complaining was all-out hell raising and abuse from her. An added burden for us kids was that we were aware that if we did have a confrontation with Mama, we knew Daddy would come to our defense. We didn't want to start a fight between them and we tried hard not to put him into the line of fire, if possible.

As in the kitchen, there were chairs and end tables in the living room, but they too hid from our view. We kids sat on the floor in front of the television because Mama did keep this area clearer than other areas. The coffee table had piles of magazines, newspapers, books, and Daddy's pipes spilling over and under it, but Mama never let the piles on it get too high.

If Daddy couldn't see over the clutter on the table, that might be a potential trigger between them, leading to a fight, so she was careful not to go too far. It was okay for her to initiate an all-out donnybrook over something she was mad about—something she could blame on Daddy, but if he initiated the fight, then the spotlight was on her—she avoided any accountability for being in the wrong. She knew how tolerant he was and she took full advantage of it to feed her compulsions to gather. The excessive number of pipes was her way of covering her other acquisitions. Because he didn't throw away the pipes she had gotten for him, she could use that as a means to make him accountable for the clutter as well.

I believe she saw this as a way to justify her purchases. Her reasoning seemed to be that if she bought something she thought Daddy might want, it would give credence to her own purchases. But why would anyone need fifty pipes? Daddy often said that Mama could find a bargain, but that her bargains were burdens in the long run because they were useless and detrimental to the household.

Mama went to bed early; she didn't care for that "old stuff on TV." She had no desire to engage with any of us about anything other than what she thought she needed. If we didn't take part in her repetition of family gossip or juicy neighborhood tidbits, then other things weren't of interest to her.

Evenings were when the rest of us experienced relatively peaceful times with Daddy. When Daddy was finished with the newspaper, I would usually look at it by laying it on the floor and getting on my knees to read it.

I started drawing the models used for clothing advertisements that commercial artists drew at that time. My interest in art was another way for me to escape the drama of my childhood.

Oscar would squeeze behind Daddy on the couch. Janis and Kitty, who was only a toddler at that time, might furrow into the mountains of clothes surrounding the rest of the living room. Roughly, four square feet of the room was passable or available for sitting. Our butts and backs made indentations in the mountains before the evening was over. Sometimes Kitty would fall asleep sucking her thumb in her cozy nest of clothes.

One thing we could count on was that most of those clothes had been clean when they were added to the top of the pile. They did smell of fresh air and sunshine for a while because Mama hung our clothes to dry. She just didn't fold them or put them away. Eventually, different items got worked to the bottom of the mountain, especially if they were clothes we weren't looking for or didn't like to wear. Only a few times did the mountain get torn down during my time at home.

We never knew what it was like to get anything from a linen closet or bathroom shelf. When we took a bath at night, it was our habit to go to the living room first to get a clean towel and washcloth off the heap. These were normally easy to find, but other clothing was more difficult to locate. We had to dig through the mountain to find underwear and socks that kept getting shifted as clothes were taken away or added.

This became another source of conflict with Mama. In our frustration to find something to wear, particularly if it was a school morning, we argued with her about navigating that fabric terrain. Our complaints landed on deaf ears or got us a hard slap from Mama's beefy arm. Again, we upset her perception of her space.

Those quiet weekday evenings were when we could talk to Daddy about almost anything. He spoke about current events, local politics, history, and geography. We saw what was going on in the world we occupied through his eyes. Daddy gave us insight into his philosophy of life.

He instilled in each of us the notion that all men are equal and that we should treat others the way we wanted to be treated. He regaled us with stories from his childhood and about the places he had been and the people he knew. Those were the times that Daddy told us we could be anything we wanted—the sky was the limit. He encouraged us to do well in school but never demanded that we had to make certain grades or achieve specific goals. His quiet encouragement made us want to make him proud.

Although Daddy was not physically demonstrative toward us as we grew older, he had been when we were infants and preschool children. As we grew, he seemed uncomfortable kissing, hugging, or telling us he loved us. Essentially, he was a shy, reserved person.

I believe that when he was sober he realized that demonstrations of affection would cause us to be in jeopardy. Any attention we got from him vexed Mama and her jealousy flared. When he drank, it was easier for him to verbalize his love and offer affectionate hugs. At those times, he also didn't care if he pissed Mama off with his declarations of devotion to his kids.

For my siblings and me, there was never any doubt that Daddy loved us and deeply cared about our well-being. We all agree that if we hadn't had Daddy in our lives, we don't know what would have happened to us. Had he abandoned us to have some sort of life for himself, we would have been more vulnerable to Mama's abuse and open to juvenile delinquency, alcohol, or drugs. His love for us was sacrificial. He wasn't perfect and he made mistakes, but he did the best he could with what he had.

Daddy assigned our schedule for going to bed. As we got older we were allowed to stay up with him to watch television or read until about nine or ten o'clock. Our house wasn't that big, so none of us ever knew what real privacy was about until we were adults. There were two bedrooms on the front of the house with a very short hall separating them. The bathroom was off the hall, across from the only closet in the house.

Janis and I shared the middle bedroom, which was about ten by twelve feet. When we originally moved into the house, we had been given an inexpensive blond bedroom suite consisting of twin beds, a mirrored dresser, and a chest of drawers. The beds were pushed up together along the outside wall, creating one big bed. The dresser was placed parallel to the beds against the inside wall and the chest of drawers was behind the door to the hallway.

Since the bedroom was central to the house's floor plan, everyone had to pass through our bedroom to get to the hall. The bathroom and Mama and Daddy's bedroom could only be reached through our room. It was not an ideal place for two teenage girls.

Janis and I weren't able to get any use from the dresser, even after putting clothes in the drawers, because Mama immediately began stacking quilts and boxes on top of it. She also placed chairs and other pieces of furniture around it and stacked things on them as well, until the chest was lost for years at a time.

There may have been some nightstands at the end of our beds but I don't recall seeing them after the first year in the house, because they too got stacked with quilts, blankets, and clothes. Not one inch of available space in our home was allotted to anyone but Mama.

By the time Janis and I were teenagers, we had one enduring wish. Apart from any childish or juvenile desire for toys or clothes, we longed to have a bed in a room where we could get out of it, walk around it, and then make it up. Janis tried to keep her part of the room straight and neat to the best of her ability, but the space was usurped by Mama or me, causing Janis a great deal of anger.

The ironic aspect of Janis's and my existence that repeated until we left home was that when we went to stay with other relatives or friends, we cleaned house for them to earn money. During the holidays, we would stay with Aunt Mary or Maw Maw Lavinia and clean their houses or iron their clothes for days at a time. We weren't even allowed to wash more than dishes at home. Even that chore was something Mama bitched about because she continually said we didn't wash the dishes the right way.

The tiny hallway leading to the bathroom and outer bedroom was only about three feet long and maybe as wide. Somehow, Mama had been able to maneuver an old dresser into that space, leaving just enough room to open the bathroom door to the midpoint of the dresser. This dresser was the kind that had drawers on both sides and an open space in the middle, which had an elongated mirror centered between two outer bifold mirrors directly above the outer drawers.

Since the dresser surface was indented, the bathroom door could be opened midway. The left inner corner of the dresser drawers caught hell from the door every time we wanted privacy in the bathroom! The placement of the dresser also blocked the only closet in the house, so it was never used.

The bathroom was tiny with only enough space for one person at a time. As kids will do, we often clogged up the toilet by excess use of toilet tissue. After repeatedly having to clear the lines, Daddy told us we needed to throw all tissue into a garbage can so the commode wouldn't get stopped up.

Mama got the largest plastic garbage can she could find to place between the wall and the commode. She wouldn't regularly empty the can. We often faced a foul smell when entering the bathroom, much like that which is experienced in a portable toilet someone may have had the displeasure to use on occasion! Eventually, we kids would take it upon ourselves to dump the can and to keep the tub and commode cleaned to the best of our ability.

Mama didn't talk to us about our bodies and maturation, but we learned about many things simply because we could see the evidence of the female condition by her haphazard lifestyle. She was neither extremely modest nor an exhibitionist, but we *still* saw more than enough for us to get clues as to what adulthood meant.

When I was about twelve, Daddy handed the newspaper to me, which was opened to the Ann Landers column. That particular day, Landers was answering a teen's question about menstruation. I ducked my head to hide my embarrassment; I could see that he was embarrassed too. He said that I should read the column and that if I had any questions I could ask Mama. I wasn't going to ask her anything. I was a prolific reader, so I understood Ann Landers's advice. Besides, a mother-hen friend from school had already filled several of us in on the birds and bees as we sat around the tetherball pole at recess.

It wasn't important to Mama to dispose of Kotex by folding and wrapping it in tissue. We all came to know what a monthly cycle was about before we even heard the word menstruation because of the bloody evidence she left in that big garbage can. She would also leave a douche bag hanging above the tub on a towel rack and bloody panties in the sink.

Often, we might find her "washing off" in the bathroom, scrubbing under her large arms with a washrag while her abundantly large breasts swung to and fro above her protruding belly. She never actually closed the bathroom door completely so it wasn't unusual to walk in on her even though it was never our intention to do so. Privacy didn't really exist in our household.

As Janis and I reached our teen years, we wanted privacy, but it wasn't always ours to have, especially since there was only one bathroom. Mama came and went as she pleased most of the time. If one of us closed the bathroom door and engaged the slide latch Daddy had installed, Mama would grab the outside knob and vigorously shake the door while screaming, "She's got that goddamned door closed tighter than Dick's hatband!" (For years, I tried to figure out who Dick was and why his hatband was tight.) Daddy respected privacy and demanded it as a matter of courtesy. Oscar and Kitty, when they were small, were just typical pesky siblings.

Oscar and Kitty didn't have their own rooms. Mama placed two full-size beds in the outer bedroom. Kitty slept with her and Daddy slept with Oscar. The room also held a couple of chests of drawers and other miscellaneous furniture Mama bought on the sly. If somebody had something to give away, Mama was the recipient.

While Kitty was growing up, Mama continued to add mattresses to their bed until they were sleeping about four feet off the floor. You literally had to use a chair to climb into the bed!

We didn't use any heat for the majority of the house in the winter. Although natural gas had been piped to all the rooms in the house, there was no space to fit a gas heater in any of the bedrooms. It was too much of a hazard for Daddy to consider installing space heaters. On cold winter mornings, Daddy got up before the rest of us to light the living room space heater and to light the oven while he could monitor them. I woke many mornings when my breath was visible in our cold bedroom. We could have used those rooms as meat lockers. The only benefit of Mama's hoarding during those years was that we could pile several of those dusty quilts on our beds to keep warm at night.

Louisiana springs and summers can be sweat-wrenchingly miserable. With no air circulating in the congested bedrooms, sleeping was a nightly fit-producing time. We used box fans to stir a little air. I habitually placed one of those fans on a chair next to my bed; I couldn't sleep when I was hot, but I paid dearly from the use of the fan with chronic ear infections and tonsillitis.

There was another room in our house that we called the drop room. This room had been an afterthought addition to the house, so we had to step down when we entered it. The doorway to this room was also accessed from Janis's and my room. This doorway was to the right as you entered our bedroom from the living room.

At one time, after Daddy moved the house onto the property, Mama's brother Robert lived with us for a short time. The drop room had a back door that opened onto the back porch. Daddy and Mama gave Uncle Robert use of this bedroom so that he was free to come and go as he chose. When Uncle Robert no longer lived with us, Mama and Daddy used the room for a brief time before moving to the front bedroom.

Eventually, it just became a junk room. This is where Mama continued to bring items into the house. For a brief period, in our early teens, Janis and I used it as a place to keep our clothes and an ironing board. Here we could listen to records or the radio. I can still see my sister with her eyes closed and her lips pursed, dancing to "Do You Believe in Magic?" by the Lovin' Spoonful. We begged Mama several times to let us have the room because it was bigger than ours was, but she made excuses as to why we couldn't have it.

I remember being mad at Mama one morning and going into that room and cranking up Steppenwolf's "Born to be Wild" as loud as I could while ironing my clothes for school. Now, every time I hear that song I think about the drop room. I think about how Janis and I wanted to make it our own special place where there would have been sunlight and a little space to move around. We craved a sense of normalcy. The only way to get it was to go to somebody else's house.

By the time I left home, I don't know if anyone was able to use that room at all. I vaguely remember that it was just dark most of the time. In it, there were boxes, chairs, clothes, dressers, and ugly dolls with brown starburst eyes and creepy, dime-store portraits of big-eyed, lost children.

At night, in the dark, the boxes took on scary shapes. I was suspicious of any noise coming from that room. Every night, I tried to close the door to the room as much as possible. There were so many old coats and dresses hung on the front and back of the door that it was next to impossible to close it completely. I didn't want to have to peer around the bulky silhouettes, trying to determine in my nearsighted way what might have been lurking there. I simply pulled the covers over my head to make it all go away.

Even in rest, there was always something shadowy looming over us, waiting for us to open our eyes in the dark. We had to try to discern what new, amorphous shape had taken over from the previous day. When would these things obliterate us and take us over? Mama certainly wasn't concerned about the situation or that her kids were exposed to dangerous living conditions.

Chapter 12

Why the Hell Hasn't This Whole Pile of Shit
Burned Down by Now?

The peace and quiet my brother, sisters, father, and I experienced while Mama was hospitalized after her breakdown was nearly the only respite we ever had. We weren't going to get a normal way of life no matter how hard we tried. I think we all just finally settled into the routine of it. It was absolutely too much to ask or to wish for that things could be any different.

We developed a high level of tolerance that may seem difficult to understand. In order to maintain levels of continuity, to exist with a daily sense of routine and peace, we had to put the clutter, disorder, and chaos out of our minds. Did we like having to live this way? Of course we didn't. But it was impossible to maintain resistance against such an overwhelmingly rigid disorder, one that we knew nothing about. The 1960s culture, presented to us by way of magazines and television was, unbeknownst to us, a superficial picture of life. Did real mothers really wear pearls to vacuum the floor? The closest thing to our reality were the folks who lived in Mayberry, USA, but even there, situations were resolved by Andy and Aunt Bea in a thirty-minute span.

Junior and senior high school were a bittersweet time in my life. I had some good friends but only a few knew the darker side of things. I buried myself in a bit of a fantasy world of books, popular music, and art, experiencing a deep longing for a different way of life. I wanted desperately to be somewhere else, to be someone else, but when I stood at the end of our driveway on Ball Cut-Off Road, I looked right and saw the same old place and the same old way of doing things and when I looked left, the world was too big then for me to see any way out.

Janis and I stayed away from home as much as we could and lived vicariously through other people's lives. We were like permanent fixtures at Carmon and Christy's house; that's the only place we felt normal. Janis and Carmon developed a deep bond, spending most of their time out of school together.

At school, I was the good friend, the one who could be counted on to tell troubles to or to help with a project. I babysat or cleaned other people's homes to make a little money and to sidestep Mama as often as possible.

A distant, family cousin lived on the corner of Ball Cut-Off across the road from Maw Maw Linnie's property. I spent much of my time away from home with that cousin's daughter, Delores. She was a few years older than I. Being an only child, she often wanted company. She called me "Brain" and paid me to help her clean house or to do school reports for her. I loved to spend the night at her house and pretend that I belonged there, sleeping in her French provincial canopy bed.

Mama never minded if Janis and I stayed away from home, especially if she thought we were doing something to earn money. Her goal was to see if she could somehow talk us out of anything we earned or force us to use it for our personal necessities. I babysat all through junior and senior high school; Mama's hand was out every time I got paid.

As I remembered this, the thought seemed harsh—didn't Mama do something at some time for me that held no expectation? I suddenly remembered that she had helped me when I was on one of my endless diets one summer. For part of that time, when I came in from babysitting, she had a broiled beef patty, sliced tomatoes, and a cold Tab waiting for me when I got home. *Well*, I thought, *she did do something for me*, and I felt slightly guilty for a few moments. It then occurred to me that even if she didn't outright demand some money from me, she would sweet-talk her way into getting me to loan her twenty bucks here or there. The prepared meals had only been a prelude to getting what she wanted.

Janis and I became much closer during the teen years. She was a bit on the rebellious side. A favorite pastime of hers was to go to the Skater's Paradise skating rink on Friday and Saturday nights. She loved going; she could skate well. It seemed to me that it was a release to her to be able to hit that hardwood floor with some song, such as the cult hit "The Letter" by the Box Tops, playing loudly on the jukebox as she whirled around energetically. I fondly recall how her face reflected determination and her body became energized when the song's lyrics, "Give me a ticket for an aeroplane/Ain't got time to take a fast train" blared out loud enough to be heard over the monstrous, droning fan on the back wall of the rink and all the noise created by the desperate skaters.

Janis liked some of the rougher crowd that hung around. She was cute and had a good shape, nice legs, and long, dark hair that attracted the boys. I was a bit of a dump and never felt attractive to anyone, so I just sort of hung in the shadows and adopted my hippie-wannabe persona.

We would arrive at the rink around six o'clock at night and stay until nine or ten. For a good portion of our teen years, this was the way we spent most Friday and Saturday nights—that was our only form of entertainment.

Janis and I often walked south on US 165 to the rink that was a good four miles from our home. Sometimes Mama would drop us off or we would bum a ride with Carmon or Christy, who would sometimes go to the rink as well. They had begun driving and dating and were having more well-rounded teen years than we were, so they weren't always available to spend the weekends with.

Going to the skating rink was something that Janis and Carmon did especially have in common. Often, the two of them would have spent hours getting ready to go flirt with the boys. Long and straight was the popular, preferred way for teen girls to wear their hair. All of us rolled our hair with big magnetic rollers or orange juice cans—that gave our hair body. But right before leaving, we thought it was a good idea to iron our hair straighter. This grooming chore was always better done if you had a buddy to help. (Janis and I often went to Carmon and Christy's house to get ready before going out.) We would get down on our knees, place as much of our hair on the ironing board as we comfortably could and then our partner would place waxed paper on top of the hair and iron away. It's remarkable to think about how many times we did this without burning ourselves up!

Janis and I spent many, many lonely times together bemoaning the way things were and plotting a way out. Almost every day, when the weather was good, we walked the black-topped Ball Cut-Off Road or walked the railroad tracks and talked about what we were going to do when we were able to leave home.

One afternoon Janis and I were home alone. Mama and Daddy, Kitty, and Oscar had gone to town. It was late spring or early summer and the house was getting warmer with each passing day. Janis and I were in the living room feeling bummed out because we didn't have anything to do. We had no way to go anywhere and no money to do anything.

Janis was eating what we referred to as a lunchmeat sandwich. I was playing with a box of kitchen matches—a favorite pastime of mine. I liked to strike one of the matches and then hold the tip of another one to it until they fused as one. Sometimes, I could actually get four or five to fuse together, creating a star shape.

I was feeling particularly morose that afternoon and had a don't-give-a-shit attitude about everything. While staring intensely at the burning matches, I made a remark to Janis that caught her off guard.

She was seated in some type of swivel rocker pushed up against the latest mountain of clothes. She was wearing cut-off jean shorts, her long tan leg casually thrown over the arm of the chair. I told her that I didn't believe what they taught us in science class.

She asked, "What?"

I said, "You know, spontaneous combustion."

She asked what I meant. I answered by asking her to stick her hand in the center of the clothes behind her head. Janis did as I asked.

"Do you feel how hot it is in there?"

She replied, "Yeah, so what?"

"Well," I said, "if there is such a thing as spontaneous combustion, why the hell hasn't this whole pile of shit burned down by now?"

She started laughing and said, "Hmm, I don't know!"

Feeling decidedly bold, I commented that maybe I should just throw those burning matches on top of the clothes to see what would happen.

She said, "You don't have the nerve, but it would be an answer to a prayer."

With that, she looked at the crust of her partially eaten sandwich and without looking back, chunked it high over her head. It landed dead center on top of the mountain. I was shocked for a second at her gesture.

We stared at each other. We got tickled. We started laughing until we couldn't stop.

At that moment, I somehow knew we would be all right. We had Daddy, we had each other, we had our music on the radio, our records, and we had laughter. Those things shored us up and kept us going forward.

One of our closest and dearest friends during our late teen years was Sandy Melder. She lived over on Clines Road next to our uncle Ray's old place. Janis and I were always made to feel welcome in her home. She knew how things were in our home and accepted us as we were. Her home became another refuge for Janis and me.

Her mother, Gwen, worked as an accountant; she left Sandy in charge when she wasn't there. Gwen never seemed to mind us hanging out with Sandy when she was away at work. At Sandy's house, we learned how to fold towels neatly and how working families pulled together. In the late afternoons, Sandy often prepared dinner for her mom, dad, and brother—Janis and I liked to pitch in and help her.

After Sandy started driving, she was our savior in that we could depend on her to give us rides when we needed them. She'd pick Janis and me up in her little Toyota without expecting gas money and without passing judgment on us for not having much money or for where we lived.

We'd make the rounds of the fast-food franchises in Alexandria on Friday and Saturday nights with her at the wheel. Somehow, we always ended up back out at the Skater's Paradise before going home around ten o'clock. Sometimes we would go to the drive-in theater, taking our own popcorn and Sandy's infamous green olives and dill pickles. Later, I depended on Sandy during our first year of college to have a ride to school, since we both commuted.

Janis taught herself to drive by getting behind the wheel of whatever vehicle might have been in our driveway. She'd sneak the keys and go crank the car or truck and back it up and then pull it forward; she'd repeat that process repeatedly. Her perseverance allowed her to know how to handle a vehicle, whether it had a standard or automatic transmission. When Janis and I did start driving—and she did way before I was brave enough to—we rarely had enough money to put gas in the car. It didn't take much; five dollars back then would take you a long way.

Even before I went to high school, Daddy had allowed me to sign off on our report cards, if for some reason he wasn't home when they needed to be signed. I could expertly forge his name. Mama rarely signed her name to anything important, unless Daddy or one of us had explained to her what the document said. It became easier for me to take care of those needs. Daddy turned to me to do this because

I was the oldest; he looked to me to be responsible for my siblings. I think I was an old soul by the age of eight.

Daddy would even let me write out checks at the local convenience store, the A&G Timesaver. The manager knew us well, so if I went in with a presigned check from Daddy, he would accept me filling in the amount for our purchase.

I got a little heavy-handed with that practice when Janis and I needed gas money. I wrote a few checks in rapid succession for gas without telling Daddy I was doing so. They bounced. The manager called Daddy to make them good. When Daddy said he hadn't written any there, the manager told on me. Daddy made me go back to pick up the bad checks as punishment, but he didn't chastise me too badly. He just said that the next time I needed to get something that I should let him know so that he could make sure there was enough money to cover the purchase.

Janis and I periodically went to Maw Maw Lavinia's on the weekends and for longer periods during the summer months. Even though she didn't like us much, just as we didn't like her, there we gained a sense of freedom from the chaos at home. She didn't pay much attention to us, which allowed us a chance to explore different parts of Alexandria and pretend we didn't live the way we did. Downtown and the Garden District streets of brick were particularly fascinating to us. The sterile cityscape of concrete sidewalks, overpasses, and paved streets held a certain appeal to us. It was foreign, fresh, new, and clean.

We could cover city concrete blocks in rapid order because our feet had been toughened from walking on asphalt roads. After all, we had spent years popping those tar bubbles with our tough bare toes. The city of Alexandria posed no threat to us; our curiosity and desire to learn other ways of being was far too strong for us to be afraid.

Although neither of us ever specifically voiced it, I think Janis and I both entered a fantasy world of "what might be" once we were unshackled from our childhood bondage to Mama. One day we would be able to shop in the nice stores and eat at the nice restaurants and nobody would know where we came from or how we got there. Those days were magic and we were so bold and unafraid. Our bond of love kept us sane. Our country innocence carried us far and a universal soul protected us.

Chapter 13

We All Still Lived the Lie

Our family attitude had evolved to a place where we all just more or less accepted the way Mama behaved. It did us no good to protest with any regularity. During my teen years, she had become more socially active than in previous years and would go on outings with Lee Rayner or go visit her sisters frequently. We all still lived the lie.

If someone did come to our house, Mama would quickly ask him or her to sit in chairs she kept under the trees in the front yard or on the porch. Everyone who came to our house seemed to accept this custom; nobody pushed the issue. It was as if we all were in on this collective secret. There was this big, white elephant in the middle of the room that no one was brave enough or assertive enough to mention.

Having people sit outside only occurred in summer, and if, God forbid, anyone came to the house during the winter, we kids would run like chickens. We were fearful that if Daddy or Mama opened the door, the person or persons would be able to see inside the house.

Mama wouldn't allow anyone to come in. I suppose she didn't want anyone outside the family to ask questions regarding the way she kept house. She knew that the way she lived was not as it should be, but she would not talk about it ever. She looked to us to keep her secret. You could see it in her eyes: it was as if they were saying, *don't betray me, and don't mention it.* Sometimes that look was sad and pathetic, but most often it was defiant and threatening. That secret drove me further and further into a push-me, pull-you relationship with Mama that lasted well into my adult years.

I had no illusions about my life as a teenager. Those weren't the glory days. I would never want to repeat that time. It was difficult for me to feel that I fit in on many levels. Living under heavy clouds gave me the sense of living two different lives. I was one way at school, sometimes a quiet, shy, decent student who liked to draw, or a slightly outspoken, verbally rebellious dreamer ranting about social injustices, like the Vietnam War and segregation, which raged at that time. But I was too afraid to draw much attention to myself.

I stayed away from home as much as I could. I found surrogate mothers—the mothers of my friends. When I did go home, to my real life, I retreated into myself by reading or listening to music or waged holy war with Mama. I didn't like her and she didn't like me. Love never entered the picture.

The ever-present tension between the two of us intensified the older I got. I became the instigator for change. Janis and I longed for that normal life we saw all around us. Nobody we knew lived the way we did. Nobody.

Most people in our area were low-income folks: some just struggling to pay the bills and feed the family; some may have hit the very lowest rung of the middle-income bracket and appeared well off compared to us. But none of these families lived in homes as we did. When other mothers invited me into their homes (and their lives) and then complained of a messy house, I just smiled and wished for their mess.

The more opportunity I had to see other existences, the more I wanted us to have that same life. I started imploring Daddy to let us do something to bring order to the house.

I got bold the summer of 1969; I was sixteen. (While the rest of the world was buzzing about that summer being the "summer of love," it wasn't in our household.) I figured that if Daddy would back us up, we could do the work ourselves and clean up the house. After all, Janis and I had become adept at the house-cleaning business—we even moved Maw Maw Lavinia's whole houseful of furniture by ourselves using a furniture dolly to load Lee's pickup.

It took me a while to convince Daddy that we needed to do this. Finally, he agreed. Daddy was a wise man and I know that he knew what was coming.

I gathered the troops in secret. I told Janis, Oscar, and Kitty that we would need to stand together and hang tough. All of us knew that it was not going to go well, but we were determined. One sunny, hot morning we confronted Mama.

"We're going to clean the house," I said.

"What do you mean?" she asked.

"I said, we're going to clean the house."

"No, y'all leave my stuff alone; I'll pick up when I get time."

"No, Mama, you'll never get time, so we're going to do it for you."

"I can't let y'all fool with my stuff. Y'all will throw all my good stuff away, just like your Daddy, Marbeth, and Shirley did when I was in the hospital."

"I can't help it, Mama. We're all tired of living like this, so you might as well get used to it. We're going to do this!"

I faced her head-on; there was no turning back in my mind. It was now or never. I was bold but scared to death as I picked up trash to throw in a garbage can. Daddy, Oscar, Janis, and Kitty were quietly working in the background.

I was Mama's target. She knew I had instigated the whole episode. She kept insisting to Daddy that he make me stop. But knowing what was in store, he had armed himself by downing a couple of beers. He had to steel himself to face her rage and to have the courage to tell her no.

Once she knew we were serious, she went into overdrive. I had prepared myself for the full onslaught. She pushed me, she shoved me, she grabbed me by the arm, she slapped at my back and shoulders, but I fended off her blows and shoved things into paper sacks and garbage cans.

Mama cried and cussed, cajoled and pleaded as we turned deaf ears and hearts to her begging. She followed us from room to room with threats one minute and promises the next. Her usual ability to outmaneuver us and wear us down wasn't working that day. We were a united force she couldn't handle. By midday, she was breaking and had to use her wild card. She broke again. Catatonia brings bliss.

Daddy took her to Central Hospital for a second time. My siblings and I were a bit shaken by the outcome, but still determined. He came back late in the afternoon without Mama. The doctors admitted her to the hospital again. We worked until dark. We were tired but eager for the promise of normalcy the next morning might bring.

Daddy was up early the next day, already burning trash, before all of us kids were up. It is amazing how united we were. Eight-year-old Kitty worked just as hard as we did. The job was daunting when I think about how we worked with nothing more than oscillating fans that only stirred the dust and did us no good unless we stood directly in front of them. We didn't have time for that; there was too much to do.

Our first priority was the kitchen. There was an unspoken need to prepare a meal and to sit together to eat it. We worked with an agenda and a vengeance.

Janis and I stayed inside while Daddy, Oscar, and Kitty cleaned the chest-type freezer on the back porch. Mama had filled the freezer to the brim with food that was now outdated or freezer burned and no longer edible. Daddy's solution was simple—he simply threw it out into the yard. Our dogs, cats, and others from the neighborhood waited patiently for the big thaw.

We conversed in spurts or not at all. Occasionally, one of us would holler after finding something we hadn't seen in a while or didn't know we had. At one point, I was cleaning out the refuse under a folding table next to the stove, trying to sort through the worthiness of various pots and pans. Janis was working on the refrigerator. I squatted down in order to reach under the table. Boxes and garbage cans surrounded me.

As I pulled empty bread wrappers, paper bags, and newspapers out from under the table, I started noticing finely shredded, multicolored papers in all the pots I pulled out.

I was puzzled about what I was seeing. I thought it might have been some sort of packing material. The more paper I found, the more puzzled I became. Finally, with stinging sweat pouring into my eyes I reached the source. A large cast-iron Dutch oven sat on the floor filled with the multicolored shreds of paper.

Cautiously, I brushed the papers away. When I heard the squeals, I stopped using my hand and grabbed for a spatula. The spatula helped me to reveal a squirming mass of pink bodies at the bottom of the pot. I couldn't believe my eyes! It was disgusting.

I called for Janis to come see. Immediately, she ran screaming to Daddy.

I'll never forget Daddy picking up that pot of shrieking mice and tossing it into the yard—or the sound those creatures made when the cats pounced.

Later that afternoon my aunt Jettie and her youngest daughter, Sandra, came wheeling into our driveway as Janis and I were making a trash drop by the side of Ball Cut-Off Road.

They didn't get out of their truck; they said what they needed to say in the comfort of the air-conditioned cab. Sandra, my outspokenly bold cousin, and I had a few things in common, but not about this particular subject. She let me know how terrible I was at being a daughter. How horribly I was treating my poor Mama, who couldn't help it.

I was ready for a fight. I lashed back at them about how they had no idea how things were in our house and what Mama put us through every day. I told them that Mama wouldn't even let them come into our house and that they knew it was true but wouldn't help us do anything about it. I screamed at them that they could have cared less about what we were feeling.

Finally, after wasted minutes of mind-numbing, useless arguing, I challenged them to get out of the truck to come help us. Quickly, they said they would never be part of getting rid of Aunt Chrissie's stuff and that we should be ashamed. God was going to make us pay for what we were doing! At that, I turned my back on them and marched back into the house.

Later that evening, Daddy went to the grocery store and bought food. Janis and I asked him if we could make spaghetti for supper and he agreed. He brought the groceries into the now-clean kitchen.

Janis and I weren't sure how to prepare spaghetti, but we gave it our best shot. We used Italian seasoning to spice it up more than Mama ever had. Daddy bought salad ingredients and an avocado, which had never been in our home before. We even had french bread to go with the meal.

All five of us, Daddy, Janis, Oscar, Kitty, and me sat down and ate that meal together. We talked, laughed, and felt like a family for an hour one hot summer evening. Those were the memories we wanted to make, the kind of memories we longed for.

The summer of 1969 was the last time my family had any solidarity while I lived under the roof of my parents' home. Mama came home all too soon. She wasn't docile this time. She was pissed and probably rightfully so. We didn't understand her need to keep those things. We didn't know that to get rid of her possessions would make the situation worse. We didn't know the correct way to handle her illness. We didn't know that she needed to be part of anything that could bring about change.

Mama's obsessive-compulsive hoarding had evolved to an even stronger urge by the time I left home at age nineteen.

Chapter 14

This Would Never Be My Home Again

By the end of my first year in college at Louisiana State University at Alexandria, I could feel my mother's hatred like a palpable presence when I entered the house.

The tension was omnipresent—even when I left the house, I knew what would be waiting when I got home.

I've sometimes wondered why it is so difficult for those of us who have known extreme conditions in the home to escape them. I think we become fearful of the unknown; I suppose it is easier to deal with the enemy you know than the one you don't. For myself, I know that my personality was tempered by living in a perpetual state of hypervigilance. I was ever watchful for what might come next, always prepared for the hammer to drop. I lived for myself between the bad times and the times when not much happened.

Mama's hoarding had grown exponentially. She was going to show us that we couldn't win against her need. For the most part, we gave up. It was something we endured in order to survive. The pleas to clean up became bickering and petty arguments about all other kinds of everyday nonsense, anything but the real issue.

I was nineteen, dating Johnny LaCour (who would later become my first husband), and working a summer aid job at the VA hospital. Mama kept tabs on every move I made. She asked me for money every time I got paid. The tension between the two of us seemed to heat up daily, as did the temperature that summer. Mama made frequent declarations about how much she hated my boyfriend and how she was going to get him arrested for various things.

About midsummer, I came home one evening in Johnny's car. Mama was mad as usual about anything I did. She kept nagging until she picked a fight. She threatened to go smash the windows out of the car. She was very jealous that Johnny would allow me to use his vehicle. She made every effort to keep me from bringing it home; this night was no exception.

Later that night when she had gone to bed, I felt free to vent my frustrations with Daddy about how she had been behaving toward me. He listened to me whine for a while.

He responded to me, but in a way that caught me completely off guard. Daddy usually sympathized with my frustrations. Some of the hardest words I ever had to hear came from his lips that evening. He said he knew how bad things were between Mama and me, but that he was powerless to stop it.

"She thinks you're happy and she will do everything in her power to destroy your happiness," he told me.

As he continued, he said he thought Mama viewed us kids as her possessions. She felt threatened and she was going to come out fighting.

He said, "I'm going to tell you the hardest thing I've ever had to say. I've always told you that you are my number-one child; don't ever forget it.

"You know your grandmother told me that when your children are little, they step on your toes and when they're older, they step on your heart. I don't want it to be this way, but you're going to have to go.

"Because if you don't, she's going to kill you and then I'm going to have to kill her. I don't want that to happen to either one of us."

I was stunned. I cried from the depths of my soul, not because I thought my daddy no longer loved me, but because I knew how much he did.

He wasn't drinking when he talked to me and that made his words all the more serious. Obviously, he had seen the way things were playing out between Mama and me. He must have been plagued by fears of how the situation might conclude itself in some horrendous tragedy.

I didn't leave right away. Johnny and I had been talking about marriage but had no definite plans at that time because individuals under the age of twenty-one couldn't marry in the state of Louisiana without the signature of both parents. Daddy warned me that Mama would refuse to sign simply to be spiteful. Johnny and I had tentatively talked of going across the Texas line where a person could marry at age eighteen.

Coincidentally, the emancipation of eighteen-year-olds in Louisiana came that summer; it turned out that I wouldn't have to have my parents sign for me to marry. Johnny and I made minimal plans to marry sometime in late August before the new semester started.

By early August, the animosity and tension between Mama and me had filtered over to the other kids as well. Janis had graduated high school and had gotten her first job at a local car dealership.

She and I owned a Chevrolet Vega that we had purchased after being passengers in a bad auto accident when we were still in high school. She used the car more than I did, especially to go to work.

Mama started the weekly habit of pilfering the car keys from Janis' purse or clothes every Friday evening while Janis was getting ready to go out. Janis said she had to play a blackmail game with Mama every time she wanted to leave the house on the weekend. Mama would give the car keys back to Janis if Janis gave her money from her weekly paycheck.

Kitty and Oscar stayed away from home more and more frequently to escape the war of words that flew throughout the house if Janis and I were home. It wasn't safe for anybody to be there at that time. Mama would rage at both of us, but mainly me—I had gotten to the point where I just couldn't tolerate her anymore. I made sarcastic remarks and back talked as my way of lashing out at her.

Everything came to a head early in August. I came home one afternoon from work to find Mama waiting for me. Daddy wasn't there, so I had no backup.

Before I could get into the door, she accosted me about wanting money. I told her I didn't have any to give her. I didn't want her to know that I had been saving the bulk of my check for when Johnny and I married.

Somehow, she found out that we had opened a savings account. The bank was giving pieces of china every time someone made a savings deposit. I swear, we sometimes thought Mama had the powers of a witch, the way she could figure out things.

She badgered me about the china. "Where are you keeping it? I bet his old mama has it at her house! You ain't helping me do a thing around here! I cook, I wash your clothes, and you need to pay me to live here."

The tirade was endless. No amount of arguing, smart-ass comments, or pleading could get her off me that day.

Suddenly, she jerked my purse off my arm and tried to go through it. I grabbed my purse back and a tug-of-war began. She eventually pushed me backward, causing me to fall over a chair stuffed with sheets and towels.

I got up and went to the bedroom. Janis was in there, trying to avoid the fray.

She mouthed, "What the hell's going on?"

At that point, I didn't care if Mama heard or not, so I told Janis loudly, "I don't know what the hell is going on, but our mother is obviously crazy."

Before Janis could warn me, Mama was on me with a vengeance. She had a wire clothes hanger in her hand. Mama used it to beat me across the top of my back and shoulders.

Daddy's words flashed through my mind. I thought, *This is how it ends.* I bent down over the bed and used my arms to shield my head.

She screamed out at me in her rage and frustration, "I'm going to show you who runs the show around here. You think you're too good to get your ass whipped, but I'll show you. You ain't grown up yet!" Mama used the hanger to emphasize each of her words.

I was screaming and crying hysterically.

Janis tried to push her off me.

Mama didn't stop until her anger was spent. Finally, she left the room.

My shoulders ached and burned. Tears, snot, and spit oozed down my face and on to my work clothes. Janis stood petrified—she didn't know what to do.

I pushed myself up and felt very clearheaded. I looked at Janis through my swollen eyes and asked her to get me an A&P grocery box out of the kitchen. Her eyes told me that she knew what was coming.

I packed everything of value I owned in that world into that cardboard box. Mama didn't interfere as I threw my meager belongings into the box. I think she knew she had finally crossed that invisible line between the two of us.

Once or twice, she shouted from the kitchen, "You better not take anything that belongs to me!"

When I finished, I asked Janis to take me to the convenience store near our house so that I could call Johnny to come get me.

I had to steer the bulky box and myself around the junk in the living room to avoid getting near Mama as I left. She sat at the end of the couch holding a cigarette up in the air, her elbow resting on a stack of clothes. She was staring at the ceiling; her right leg was crossed over the left, swinging ferociously back and forth, indicating to me how agitated she was.

I waited until I got to the door before turning back. Janis waited on the porch for me, keys in hand. I turned to Mama and said, "I'm leaving."

I suppose I wanted her to tell me she was sorry for treating me the way she had or to beg me not to go. I allowed the little girl inside me, she who lived in a fantasy world of wishing for a sense of normalcy, to hope for a few seconds.

Mama said, "Go on and see if I care."

It took me a few months to adjust to having left home. I would sit at night in the big claw-footed bathtub of our first apartment in Alexandria and cry so that Johnny wouldn't see me. I missed home, but I had to keep asking myself why I was missing that place.

Late in October, I went out to Ball to visit my family, hoping that would help me release the deep melancholy feeling that would overwhelm me at night. I was missing my sisters, my brother, and my daddy. Mama didn't give me an opportunity to leave home with any kind of blessing or hope for the future.

As I entered the living room, Daddy greeted me with a big smile. Mama wouldn't stay in the room. I sat precariously on the end of the couch, feeling uncomfortable and ill at ease. I felt the heat of the room pressing down on me and saw that nothing had changed in the three months I had been gone, except for the addition of some more plastic flowers and pictures on top of the TV.

I felt the weight of the place more than I ever had. It was more than oppressive. I looked at Daddy and felt this tremendous surge of empathy for him. I could leave, I could escape, but he could not. My resentment toward and my dislike of my mother peaked at that moment. I didn't care if I ever saw her again.

I felt at that time that Daddy had voluntarily made himself a prisoner of Mama's illness. He knew that his children could find the freedom to become whatever they were meant to become. But he wasn't going to abandon her no matter how bad things got.

We finished our conversation about mundane things; I knew it was time for me to go. I couldn't wait to get back out into the coolness of that fall evening. I felt tremendous sadness, relief, and release. This would never be my home again.

Chapter 15

She Wasn't Going to Forget What We Did—
We Would Pay for It

Once Janis and Oscar left, Daddy saw the hopelessness of the situation in the old house. I believe he knew that Mama had reached a point of no return. No amount of reasoning or his threats to leave could budge her from her position.

In turn, Daddy's position became one of "If you can't beat 'em, join 'em." He came up with a solution he thought might solve Mama's hoarding. He told Mama she could continue to collect things, but instead of bringing the items home, they would make a business of it. Daddy rented a storefront building at Kingsville and told Mama to have at it.

It didn't take her long to fill the place up. Mama had an unnervingly weird, magnetic ability to be the recipient of cast-off goods. She bought clothing and household goods cheaply at garage sales and thrift stores to supply her business. Sometimes people simply dropped off unwanted merchandise. Mama seemed to put out invisible signals to the world that she would take anything other people no longer wanted. It didn't matter what those things were. She might not even know what some of the items were, let alone how to use them.

Daddy and Mama opened the resale shop four or five days a week. A problem arose when Mama was alone. When someone came in to make a purchase Mama jacked the prices so high that the potential customer left disgusted. It was easy to blame failure of the business on people not wanting to pay what she asked. By maintaining high prices, she could hang on to what she valued. This was heaven for her—she could come in every day, look at this vast array of stuff in the cavernous store, and know that it was hers.

If, by some stroke of luck, some naïve customer happened to pay the exorbitant prices she set, then she would revel in her good fortune. Money in her hand or purse was a huge turn-on for Mama. That money also supplied her with the necessary means to purchase more things.

Soon, Daddy had to pay rent on what had essentially become a high-priced storage unit. They couldn't afford to keep up the charade—Daddy's income was limited. He closed the business down. The idea might have worked had Daddy spent every moment with Mama to monitor her business practices. No matter how good Daddy's intentions were, he couldn't spend that much time with Mama—no one could.

By then, Kitty had become a teenager. Oscar had joined the National Guard; he was stationed away from home. Daddy missed having all his kids around. It was difficult for Janis and me to visit with them on a regular basis. When we did go, Mama relegated us to the chairs under the sweet gum trees as she did outsiders.

Janis and I worried about Kitty and the kind of teenage life she would experience. We invited her to spend time with us in our homes as often as she was willing to come.

Daddy often came to see me, to talk about the ongoing situation with Mama. He was worried about the deteriorating old house. When anything broke down, it was almost impossible to reach the source of the problem because there were too many things blocking the way. An old house that had been renovated couldn't last forever if routine repairs and maintenance weren't done. Any emergency repairs were usually done by him as a way to save money and as a way to save face. How could he explain to a repairman that he couldn't reach a particular section of his own house because it was blocked by clothes or boxes?

In a somewhat desperate maneuver—desperate because Daddy really couldn't afford a mortgage—he decided to buy a mobile home. When he discussed that possibility with Johnny and me, I could sense the underlying excitement he was feeling. Daddy had talked to a mobile-home distributor. He told us that he could buy the home with very little money down. The monthly payments, he thought, were manageable.

During the 1970s, many folks were purchasing mobile homes as a solution to not being able to afford to build. Mobile homes were the rage throughout rural central Louisiana for young couples starting out or older couples who couldn't keep up the old home place.

Daddy's solution presented an opportunity for him, Kitty, and Mama to have a fresh start. He expressed that he would like for at least one of his kids to feel a sense of normalcy during their teen years by being able to have friends over. Daddy hoped to afford Kitty that opportunity. He had also sensed that Mama had become overwhelmed by the amount of stuff in the house. He saw it as being next to impossible to get her to agree to eliminate some of those things.

I was excited for him and Kitty. I had a recurring thought that just maybe after all the years of living such a bizarre life that we might be able to come together as a family without embarrassment or reproach. I was hungry for a feeling of connection again. My fantasies of the ideal family loomed large. Janis and I could now bring our husbands over to visit or have supper with Daddy, Mama, and Kitty. We could finally go home for holidays or other important events.

Daddy planned everything out. He took Mama and Kitty with him to pick out the mobile home. They were able to pick the floor plan and interior colors they liked. Kitty would have her own bedroom with attached bath on the kitchen end of the mobile home.

Daddy told the guys who pulled the mobile home to his lot to move it directly in front of the old house. When I think of it now, I realize that this was perhaps his geographic solution to the problem of trying to deal with Mama. Just as Janis and I thought that by relocating, we could rid ourselves of the frustration of having to look at or deal with Mama's disorder, he too had reached a point where the only relief available to him was to leave it all behind.

I remember Kitty's excitement about having her own small bedroom with its brown paneled walls and adjoining half bath. The gold appliances, textured green-and-white-kitchen wallboard with a tree branch design, faux stone paneling on the living room wall with matching pewter sconces, and the almond-colored tub, sinks, and toilets were the height of '70s décor. It was an odd feeling to see Mama and Daddy in that setting, but that feeling was encased with a degree of hope.

Their move into the new place was relatively easy and uneventful, and blessed peace reigned for a while.

During my twenties, Mama and I developed a better relationship than we ever had. At this time in her life, she was enthusiastic about getting out and about. She maintained a certain lightheartedness that had not been present since I was a toddler. She wore decent, clean clothes and made an effort to be presentable when she went places.

I'm not sure if my attitude toward her had changed; perhaps she sensed that it had. We managed to spend time with each other without the old animosity surfacing. I still had trouble with her manipulative spirit and judgmental gossip, but I wasn't living in the same house with her anymore. I gained a certain amount of tolerance toward her for a time.

As the years slipped by after Kitty left home, Mama reverted more and more to her old ways. She became a fixture at local garage sales. Women whispered behind their hands when she stepped out of her car.

She never missed listening to a daily radio show called *The Swap Shop*; it was one of her favorite pastimes. Listeners called in with various items they had for sale or were looking to buy. If something caught her fancy, she would quickly dial the number announced on air and start negotiating with the owner.

As before, Daddy stayed away from home as much as he could. While he was away, Mama sneaked new stuff into the old house. The way the mobile home was set up, she could open the back door and go onto the steps of the house to unload her treasures. Once that room was too filled to open the door anymore, she began sneaking things into the mobile home. She started squirreling things away in Kitty's little room even before Kitty left home.

I suppose Daddy and the rest of us thought Mama would continue to collect her stuff but would have consideration for the new place by using the old house for the storage of the things she couldn't bear to part with. I suppose we fooled ourselves into believing that she would leave the mobile home alone. That wasn't to be. Within just five years of the purchase of the mobile home, Mama had it filled with useless things.

As adults, my siblings and I came together one final time to attempt to intervene in how Mama's condition was forcing Daddy to live. Everyone in the family could see how unhappy Daddy was. He had tried everything he knew to do. He hadn't pushed or forced Mama to change. Daddy diplomatically tried to work around the way she behaved.

Mama had brought so many things into the mobile home (which was only fourteen feet wide and seventy feet long) that they weren't able to use the central air and heat—she had most of the floor vents covered by excess rugs and furniture. Daddy was afraid, and rightly so, that the motor would burn up if they tried to run it.

Arguments between them erupted frequently, word reaching me through conversations Daddy had with Johnny when they went hunting or fishing.

Mama called me continually, complaining about Daddy, shifting the focus to him as the reason for their fights. Johnny prompted me to talk to Daddy about the situation. Daddy told me that she had gotten worse than he could ever have imagined with her acquisition of things. He said that no matter how much he tried to reason with her, she wouldn't listen. Now that their children were gone, Mama had more space available to fill.

Janis and Kitty were living in Texas at that time, which required us to make our plans via long-distance phone calls.

We had to plan a date in advance for a weekend they both could come to Louisiana. This time we had the backup of husbands who had grown to love Daddy as much as my siblings and I did.

None of us wanted to see him have to continue in those conditions. He was miserable. It was painful and frustrating to watch him struggle with the hoarding. Daddy had finally reached a place in his life where things should have been a little easier. He had earned the right to live in relative peace. Nobody thought it was too much to ask of Mama to rid their lives of so much stuff.

It was going to be a warm weekend. My sisters, Johnny, and I arose early to a beautiful June morning and left for the mobile home. Mama and Daddy were up, but instead of waiting for us to come to the door, Mama immediately came out onto the wooden front deck of the beige mobile home.

When she saw the group of us standing there while Oscar pulled into the driveway, a shadow of panic passed across her face.

"What are y'all doing here?" she asked.

None of us wanted to blurt out our purpose, but she had to be confronted.

At first, we thought Mama might be agreeable about letting us clean up. Although surprised to see Janis and Kitty home that weekend, she immediately began asking them about what was going on in their lives in Texas.

She wouldn't look at me or address me. With her keen radar, she could sense that something was amiss. Her attempt at banal conversation was a way to buy time, to put off the inevitable. It was obvious that she felt caught off guard, but I could also see that she was going to pull from a reserve of excuses and threats. It soon became apparent that she wasn't going to cooperate.

She kept insisting that she was going to get around to "straightening up," but she hadn't had the time to do it right—she didn't need our help.

Words of reason soon turned to words of anger, especially between her and me. But then Janis, Kitty, and Johnny added their reasons for why she needed to let us begin. We were insistent that we were going to start clearing out stuff so that she and Daddy could live in a clean environment.

A furious tug-of-war ensued. Mama was agitated and thoroughly pissed off. For every item we tried to take out, she had an argument or excuse as to why it had to remain. She didn't immediately start cursing and threatening but instead acted like a petulant child retrieving a broken toy from the garbage can.

This was the 1980s; my family had no clue as to how to effectively deal with Mama's problem. Had we known how to deal with our mother's obsessive-compulsive disorder at that point, we might have been able to help ease some of her anxiety and to help her lead a more productive and fulfilling life.

I can see now that all she saw was that her kids were aligned against her with Daddy. If there had ever been an opportunity for any of us to know what we were dealing with and to reach out for professional, therapeutic assistance over an extended period we might have had some degree of success with Mama during that period of her life. A concerted, ongoing therapy might have made a difference. We didn't know any existed.

It might have been beneficial to have had an unbiased therapist there as a mediator to assist Mama in setting goals. Someone with no emotional connection to the situation who could help monitor her anxiety level might have eased her into a more cooperative attitude. It was a moment in time that escaped us—instead, we plunged headlong into an all-out battle with a mental health condition we knew nothing about. A weekend was not enough time to tackle the problem we were so desperately trying to resolve.

Through ignorance, we tried to reason logically with her as to why so much of what she had stuffed into the mobile home needed to be disposed of. This lead to arguments and all-out screaming matches with her as each of us grew more and more frustrated and angry during the first hour or so of our intervention.

I tried to stay as quiet as possible because it was quite clear that she blamed me as being the instigator of this new and bigger assault on her turf. If looks could have killed, I would have been dead several times that morning.

Mama's agitation and anger were at full throttle. I'm sure she felt overwhelmed by our gang approach. She capitulated quickly because she couldn't manipulate us with her threats or pleas to leave her things alone. Mama called her sister Jettie to come and pick her up. She couldn't bear to endure watching her precious possessions fall to the ax of the determined men. As she walked to Aunt Jettie's car, she screamed, "I'm never gonna forget this—y'all are gonna pay for it." Mama stayed away throughout that weekend.

Once Mama left, we set to work with a vengeance. The bedrooms were situated on opposite ends of the mobile home. Mama had taken over Kitty's bedroom, the one next to the kitchen. She had not been using the small, connecting bathroom, because she had the door blocked with boxes of clothes. Kitty was appalled that this space was totally unrecognizable from the brief time she had gotten to use it. As we deconstructed layers of several years of collecting, all the things Kitty left behind were exactly where she had left them. That teen memorabilia had simply been covered by hundreds of new items Mama had piled into the little room.

None of us wore masks to protect us from the dust, mold, and mildew we stirred up. As we removed each layer of clothing, paper, plastic, and boxes, we encountered more and more grime and roach trails permeating the strata. At one point, we had to use a large push broom just to budge the layers of dirt and miscellaneous items that had shifted down to the carpet and linoleum.

Daddy, Oscar, and Johnny tried to remove the black Naugahyde couch that came with the mobile home, but because Mama had stored so many boxes of books and clothing on it, the men couldn't lift it. The interior springs had been pushed down into the floor, rendering it virtually unmovable. Eventually, Johnny asked Daddy to get an ax. Johnny chopped the couch into pieces inside the mobile home. The men moved the couch in sections out into the yard, where we burned it.

By the end of the weekend, we were all feeling the effects of the cleanup. Kitty and I both got bad sinus infections from two days of working in filth and heat. Janis worked in shorts because it was so hot in the mobile home. She developed an ugly red rash on her thighs that took a while to clear up.

At that time, we felt it was worth the effort because Daddy was pleased and happy with the results. He had commented several times during the course of that weekend about how fortunate he was to have the kids he had. Several times, he stopped to let us know how much he appreciated our efforts.

Daddy understood the gravity of our united attempt to help him; he was overcome with emotion. We felt good knowing that we were leaving him with a clean bathroom, clean sheets on his bed, and the ability to open his bedroom window for cool, clean air to breathe.

Sadly, this time was no different from before. Mama started collecting almost as soon as we were finished. It felt as if she was launching an all-out effort to show us that we were not going to win. This was her house, her territory, and she'd be damned if we were going to take anything away from her. Mama also had renewed reason to harbor resentment toward her children, especially Johnny and me.

When it was just the two of them, a sort of compromise took place. As long as Daddy had his limited amount of space to read, to write his letters to the editor, or to watch the news shows he loved so much, he ignored Mama's hoarding. He had to. That was the only way he knew to live. Daddy's expectations weren't that Mama had to keep a "nasty nice" house, which is how he referred to those who might go to extremes to keep an excessively clean environment. All he wanted was to be able to move in his home without fear of knocking some pile down on his head, to be able to find clean clothes readily, or to use a refrigerator that didn't have a nebulous jam-up of moldy, inedible food in it.

We all developed such a level of tolerance for the conditions in which we lived that I'm sure it would be worth a psychological study. I equate it to putting on psychic blinders or withdrawing into yourself in order to protect your psyche. Tuning it out was a way of being, a necessary protective stance. It was not a condition of apathy; instead, it was a forced stalemate of action.

Daddy would sit in the armchair next to the faux stone wall, his Old Milwaukee beer can perched precariously on the chair rest. Often, he wrote in a dollar-store notebook to express his feelings about politics or some adventure he had experienced in his younger days. After consuming several beers, Daddy might even call a headline-grabbing politician or the governor. He lived in isolation—a prisoner of circumstances. The obligatory pact he made with himself to look after Mama kept him from the very connections that helped make his life meaningful.

Daddy became the buffer between Mama and utter darkness. He kept the day-to-day trash taken out and made sure that they had cooked food. He kept the pathways clear as best he could so they could navigate the terrain of piles and piles of dusty clothes and objects. Daddy was there to remind Mama to eat more sensibly and to stay away from sugar as her diabetes grew worse.

Many times, he told me that he had lived a full life. He could accept that he would die before his kids, but he couldn't accept anything happening to one of us. His desire was to see that his kids were living decent lives. Daddy gave up the fight about the hoarding—it had gone on too long and he needed some sort of peace. He and Mama existed in a wobbly sort of truce in a home with no air ventilation.

The arguments that had marked their relationship were now sporadic. Daddy came and went as he pleased. He still loved to go fishing, but his hunting days were more about being in the woods with Oscar, Johnny, or my son, Patrick. Daddy taught each of them the things he knew about wildlife and the lay of the Louisiana woodlands.

Mama became more isolated. She was driving less and less. She visited her sister Jettie occasionally but mainly stayed close to home. She had a good relationship with Carmon and Christy's elderly grandmother, My Trude, who still lived across the road.

After Estelle Thibodeaux retired, Mama finally developed a relationship with her after all their years of being neighbors. Estelle's little red brick home became Mama's refuge to get out of the heat of the mobile home. For years, she spent many afternoons and evenings there, eating simple meals My Trude had cooked. Once My Trude died, Mama continued the arrangement with Estelle.

Chapter 16

Saying Good-bye to Daddy

Daddy stayed busy with little projects over the next ten years. He continued to garden on a much smaller scale than in years past. Green onions, cabbage, and mustard greens were the main things he cultivated as he got older. He had an old, rusted wheelbarrow in which he planted pink clover; he loved the way it looked as it grew and draped over the edge.

I opened a flower shop with a friend in 1988. About a year after opening, Daddy was inspired to bring me a cylinder of cedar he had cut off the end of a log. He came to my house one morning, mid-November, before I went to my shop. As he handed the piece to me, the clean scent of the freshly cut wood wafted between us. Rather shyly, he told me he thought that it was a beautiful piece of wood and that he thought I could do something pretty with it.

I smiled to myself, thinking how Daddy could see beauty in simple things. I took the wood to my shop and intentionally set out to create something Daddy would like. I sealed the wood with varnish. While it dried, I began thinking of how I wanted to design the arrangement. I decided to use dried materials—cattails, pinecones, bear grass, colorful fall leaves, and sheet moss. The design was set off by the placement of a flocked, reclining, decorative deer at the base of the arrangement. Daddy loved it; he thought it would be a great seller. It pleased me to make him smile.

Late in the summer of 1991, he started his yearly process of cutting firewood with Oscar. A few years before, he had invested in a wood-splitter so that the two of them could make extra money each year by selling the ricks of wood they cut and split before winter came. At sixty-seven, he could still split two ricks of wood a day.

Daddy was a slender, lean man who was rarely physically ill, except for yearly bouts of hay fever. His hands still shook, a sign of his emotionally fragile condition, but physical work calmed him more readily than anything else did. Other than having to have cataracts removed from one eye and the removal of an embedded sliver of steel from the other eye, Daddy basically visited the doctor only for yearly checkups.

That fall he seemed noticeably thinner. Then he started coughing. It was one of those dry, annoying kinds of coughs. It lingered longer than usual. I don't think any of us realized the seriousness of it at first; Daddy seemed to shrug it off.

Daddy finally decided to see why the cough wouldn't go away. He asked me to accompany him to the VA hospital. Blood work and a chest X-ray were ordered; the afternoon dragged.

After what seemed like hours of waiting, he was finally called back to consult with an intern. I was with him in that section of the emergency department when he received the diagnosis. The young doctor was brusque and matter of fact as he told Daddy that he had lung cancer. Daddy didn't say anything. I stood behind him—stunned and quaking inside. I was crushed and wanted to pummel the man for showing Daddy so little compassion.

The intern rudely asked, "Mr. O'Neal, how many packs you smoke a day?" Daddy didn't answer because I quickly interjected that he didn't smoke cigarettes, just a pipe. The man never acknowledged my statement.

The intern told him that he would be scheduled for chemotherapy, radiation treatments, and possibly surgery. He told Daddy to go to scheduling and then to the pharmacy for whatever meds he had been prescribed.

Daddy took the news very stoically; he seemed quietly stunned, lost in his own mind, thinking about the ramifications of the words we'd heard. We spoke little, if at all, as I drove him home that afternoon. The only thing he said with surety was that he would not undergo chemotherapy.

Once we got back to their home, I tried to explain to Mama that Daddy would need to live in a clean environment, which could potentially benefit his chances of surviving the cancer. I asked her to let me clean the mobile home so that he could have that chance. She refused.

I started to try and reason with Mama, but when I looked at Daddy and saw how defeated he looked, I knew it would do no good. I asked Daddy to come to my house until he got better. He readily agreed, which frightened me immensely. Daddy spent the last night with my mother that night.

That evening, I had a brief conference with Johnny and my children. They all rallied around Paw Paw Pat. My son, Patrick, was only eleven at the time, but he stepped up to the plate in a sacrificial, unselfish fashion and offered up his room for his grandfather. Patrick slept on a palette of blankets on the floor of my bedroom for the five months Daddy was with us.

I think I knew that day that he would not last long. He had been too easily swayed to come and live with Johnny, our children, and me. Had he felt as though he had a chance to beat the odds one more time, he would never have wanted to weigh us down with the burden of caring for him.

Aunt Kitty, Daddy's sister, had moved back to Louisiana the year before. She was supportive and offered to do whatever she could. It was a doubly sad time for us all; we had lost Uncle Wig only months before Daddy had been diagnosed.

About a month after the diagnosis, he was scheduled for surgery to remove his diseased lobe. Janis, Aunt Kitty, and Oscar and I waited hopefully but anxiously in the surgical waiting area of the VA. We expected to be there for a long period but unfortunately, the surgeon came out after only about forty-five minutes. The news was grim. The cancer had spread to the lining in Daddy's lungs—there was no way to remove it surgically. The surgeon suggested that radiation might possibly shrink the malignancy.

Daddy was in the hospital only a brief time—essentially, he had been opened up and then closed up quickly. He didn't need a long recovery. Within a few days, Daddy was able to drive himself to the VA for the daily radiation treatment runs. The VA had contracted with a radiation center in Alexandria so men who required it would be taken there daily in a little white van. The reality of his illness struck my family and me when he came home with the purple-blue radiation marks on his fragile neck and chest.

Over the course of his illness, while he was still able to take care of his business and drive, he set about finalizing his life. Purposefully and quietly, he made plans for his remains, which were to go to the Bureau of Anatomical Services located on Perdido Street in New Orleans. Independently, he had decided to give his remains to this institution so that medical interns could scientifically study them at one of the participating Louisiana schools of medicine or dentistry in New Orleans, or in Shreveport, or at Tulane University in New Orleans. Daddy hadn't wanted any of his children to be burdened with planning a funeral or absorbing the cost of one.

Just as quietly, Daddy offered to make amends to family or friends he might have offended over the course of his lifetime. He sat and wrote lengthy letters to anyone he thought he might have wronged, especially his brother Darlie, with whom he had been estranged for a few years.

He didn't ask for sympathy; he didn't wail or moan over his fate, but I sensed that he was suffering the most severe emotional pain of his life. The pain he felt was centered not on his physical pain, but rather on the pain he felt his death would cause the rest of us. Again, he was being the protective, unselfish father we knew him to be.

Ultimately, he worried about what was to become of Mama. Every day that he could drive, he would drive to the mobile home to see about her. He kept her supplied with groceries, checked the mail, took care of their business, took her to the doctor, and remained the anchor in her life. Not once did she come to my house to see about him.

I resented my mother with every fiber of my being during that awful time. I couldn't forgive her for turning her back on the man who had never turned his back on her. I didn't want to see her and I certainly didn't want to deal with her bullshit.

I lived numbly during that time. I couldn't think about Daddy being sick, about Daddy dying. I pretended for a while that this was a permanent arrangement—that Daddy would stay with us indefinitely.

I had to keep going, had to think about my three kids and their well-being, had to think about a husband who was giving up on himself, who had a roofing business but couldn't work because he had gotten hurt, had to continue making a stab at running a small business that wasn't making much money. At the age of thirty-six, I thought there was an enormous black hole in my future and that someone was going to bulldoze me into it.

Janis and her husband, Ed, came in from Houston and took Daddy to Toledo Bend for a few days. They thought he might enjoy being on the lake and maybe doing a little fishing. None of us kids knew how to deal with this tragedy; we were all devastated. We were in foreign territory; we had not lost anyone that close to us and we didn't know how to navigate the stages of a terminal illness.

Daddy was self-conscious about being in my home. He wasn't accustomed to being around kids and the hustle and bustle of a household anymore. He never complained about the noise, but I could feel that he wasn't entirely comfortable. Daddy felt heartsick that Patrick had given up his room. I believe he thought he was disrupting our routine.

His appetite wasn't very good. I cooked for him, but nothing seemed to appeal to him. I kept him supplied with Ensure so that he was at least getting some nutrition. About the only thing that he could tolerate was oatmeal or scrambled eggs. I cooked one or the other of those for him each morning.

On one particular morning, I had prepared old-fashioned oatmeal the way he liked it. I gave Daddy as big a bowl as I thought he could eat. He always shook a little salt into the cereal before he added sugar and milk. He reached for a large glass saltshaker I kept on the kitchen table. As he started to shake the salt, the green plastic lid plopped over and poured a pile of salt into his oatmeal. I turned from the sink just as this happened. I realized that one of the kids had not screwed the lid back on right and that had caused it to fall off. My heart broke when I saw Daddy's face. Tears welled in his eyes and he kept saying, "I'm sorry, I'm sorry."

I tried my best to keep my composure, to let him know that it wasn't his fault. I quickly made him another bowl. I held myself together until I got to my shop before I broke down and wept. I didn't know how to help him.

A week or so later, Daddy came by my shop unexpectedly. He wanted to let me know that he was concerned about Johnny. I stood behind my work counter and listened as he said that he felt Johnny was severely depressed. Daddy knew that it was hard on a man who had been accustomed to supporting his family not to be able to fulfill that obligation. He implored me to check into getting some help for Johnny and to enquire about his eligibility for disability Social Security.

When he left, I couldn't help thinking that he was a remarkable man. He was dying, but he felt compassion for his son-in-law and concern for me and my kids.

Near the end of January 1992, Daddy sat at my kitchen table with Johnny and me. He was weak and his appetite was almost gone. Johnny had helped him get into the bathroom that morning and then shaved him because he was too weak to hold the razor.

Looking down at the table, his hands knotted together, Daddy said he didn't think he could drive over to see about Christine anymore. He asked us to look after her.

Johnny told him, "Give it up, Pat; you've done everything you could for her, now it's time for you to be taken care of."

From then on, he didn't leave the house. A few weeks later, he stumbled out of the bedroom in his little striped pajamas, confused and nauseated. I told him I thought we better go to the hospital. I got him into the car and we left right away.

On the way there, he kept reaching down to the floorboard, making scooping motions with his hands. This scared me and I asked him if he needed something.

Daddy said, "No, I'm just trying to pick up these crawfish." I knew then that the cancer had spread to his brain. The VA hospital admitted Daddy for the last time.

For about two weeks, my sisters and brother and our Aunt Kitty would stay at the hospital each day to be near Daddy. He was no longer aware of our presence. It was hard on all of us to see him slipping away, especially Janis, who lived in Houston at the time. She would make the trip from Houston to Louisiana every weekend to see Daddy before having to make that long drive back.

Kitty came in from Fort Worth and stayed with me throughout the end of Daddy's illness. Early in the mornings, she would help me get the kids off to school and then we would go to my flower shop for a time before we went back to the hospital, where we spent the afternoons and evenings.

It became a daily routine to gather in Daddy's room with Aunt Kitty and talk about old times. We had a recurring joke about a penny that stayed on the floor under Daddy's bed. We knew the room was cleaned daily and mopped. For some odd reason that penny never got swept or mopped away. We referred to it as our penny from heaven. Somehow, the knowledge that it was there was reassuring.

The staff there was exceedingly kind to us. One of the most valuable life lessons I learned at that time was one given me by a nurse in the acute care unit. She could see how difficult accepting Daddy's impending death was to us. She wisely told us that often folks say prayers to prolong the life of a loved one, but that those prayers were selfish ones.

Continuing, she said that the prayer, asking that a loved one be relieved of suffering through death, was a hard one to pray, but one worth praying. She told us we would know when that time had come.

Neither Mama nor any of her family came to visit Daddy during this last hospitalization.

Daddy died on Saturday morning, March 8, 1992. My sister Kitty was at the hospital with me. It was an agonizing and surreal scene. We had befriended a young man who had hitchhiked from the Midwest to visit his ailing father—I don't even remember his name. Kitty and I had advocated with the hospital staff to allow him to have a place to shower. We even got them to bend the rules about sleeping in the waiting rooms so that he could spend time with his dad. He was with us that morning. The three of us stood tightly together and watched as Daddy struggled to breathe. None of us had ever been present when someone died.

Janis had not been able to come that particular weekend. I dreaded making the call to her to let her know because she dearly loved our father and wanted to be with him at the time of his death. I knew she would want to see Daddy one last time. I was fearful that the courier for the Bureau of Anatomical Services would come to retrieve Daddy's body before she could get there. I made the dreaded call; she was emotionally devastated. She and her husband left Houston immediately.

Oscar had avoided the hospital the last week or so. Of the four of us, I think he is as sentimental as our father was. To see the man he held so dear suffer and die was not something Oscar could bear. I called him—he had been on standby. Oscar had been as close to Daddy as any son can be to a father. His voice broke when I shared the news.

Our Aunt Kitty came shortly after Daddy died and she too was upset that she had not made it in time. Just seeing her there and knowing she supported us gave Kitty and me that sense of a mother figure's love; the kind of love we couldn't get from our own mother.

After calling Janis, I told both my sister Kitty and my Aunt Kitty that I would have to go get Mama. I thought that it was necessary for her to see Daddy; otherwise, she would never believe that he had died. They both agreed.

I called Mama to let her know that Daddy had died. I paused, but she didn't say anything. I said, "Mama, did you hear me? Daddy died."

The way she asked, "Oh, he did?" nauseated me. I didn't give her a chance to say anything else. I just insisted that I was driving over to get her and that she had to come back to the hospital with me. Her next question chilled me to the core: "Can you take me next week to see about widow's benefits?"

Janis, Kitty, and I had discussed the need to have some sort of service to mark Daddy's passing. We knew it would be important to provide an avenue for our family to say good-bye to Daddy and to have some sort of closure. We planned a memorial service for him at the church I attended, St. Michael's Episcopal Church in Pineville. The interim rector at that time, Father Jim Adams, was gracious and willing to accommodate our wishes, even though Daddy had not been a parishioner.

I was inspired to go over to Daddy's garden and collect some of the things he grew. I pulled up some green onions, cabbage, and pink clover, with tears falling in the dirt. With the produce I had gathered and some added blue Iris, I made a floral tribute for the church. I wanted to design it in such a fashion that when any person who attended the memorial service looked at it they would immediately be reminded of Pat O'Neal.

The morning of the service, we set a small white-linen-covered table before St. Michael's smoothly planed, honey-colored wood altar. On it, we placed a photograph of Daddy dressed in a light blue shirt and his favorite gray felt hat. Next to it, I placed the arrangement made using the products of my father's hands.

My father's family and a surprising number of friends from the community attended the service. I gave the eulogy. Janis had written a heart-wrenching letter to Daddy, to say publicly how important he had been to her. She requested that my daughter Courtney read it at the service.

It was a moving and apt celebration for a man who had influenced so many lives. It was our attempt to create a remembrance for our daddy. We saw him as the father who had tried his best to rear four children in harsh and sometimes heinous circumstances.

Uncle Darlie came up to me after the service with tears in his eyes. He gazed at the conglomeration of living plants and said, "That was Pat." Before we both could break down, he lightened the mood by requesting that when he went, he wanted me to make his arrangement out of bitter weed.

After the service, we ate a meal in the parish hall, lovingly prepared by women from the church. My brother, sisters, and our immediate families gathered at my house at the end of the day.

My mother chose not to attend.

After Daddy died, I went to the VA hospital to thank the nurses and attendants who had helped us so much to get through that difficult time. On the drive over, only a few miles from my house, I was thinking about how I had had no preparation to go through the death of someone so dear. I thought about how there were so many things I would have done differently had I known better.

Kitty and I had not been able to hold Daddy's hand in his last moments. We were afraid of the unknown. All we could do was stand there. We clung to each other as we watched him take his last breath. I would have wished that we could have laid hands on him to help him ease out of this world. If we could have soothed his brow or dampened his parched lips, I think the memory of his passing would not still hurt so much. I would have wanted to have been stronger and to have had Oscar and Janis and Kitty all with me to say good-bye to the man we loved so much.

As I made my way up the long drive, I wept for my father and for my own failings. I wept for all the things I should have done and for all the things I couldn't do to bring him some last bit of peace and joy. I sat in my car for a moment, not thinking I had the strength to go inside the building. Finally, I opened the car door.

As I placed my foot on the concrete parking lot, I gazed at the ground and through my tears; I saw a bright copper penny. I felt near my father in that moment.

My father's illness and death was one of the greatest and most painful challenges of my life. He had been my anchor and the most influential person in my life. No mere words can ever adequately express my deep and abiding love for him, or can they express how woefully lost and inadequate I was to lead my family forward.

Chapter 17

Walking to New Orleans

For a little over two years after Daddy died, Mama continued to live in the mobile home. She depended on me to take her where she needed to go and to be Daddy's replacement for important decisions. It was not an easy time. But I allowed it to happen out of a need to honor my father. One of his last requests of me was to take care of her.

Mama knew my heart as she knew Daddy's heart. It was a sick game of "crying wolf" that transpired between us, and I fell for it every time. No matter what I was doing, I dropped everything to go to her rescue. She had no consideration for my life, my work, or my children.

This would have been the time for me to get some professional help. I wanted to walk away, but guilt riddled me. My martyr complex wouldn't allow me to disrespect the memory of my beloved father. I couldn't tell anyone no—I was too emotionally weak to protect myself. It was easier to keep adding up Mama's daily offenses that made my life hell than to lay my burdens on a professional. I understand now that I was also influenced by the time and the culture I occupied. After all, Mama wasn't barking mad. She hadn't pulled Daddy's old 12-gauge shotgun out to take potshots at passersby. Except for continually pulling on me, she was by all appearances functional.

How was I to explain to anyone that I needed help dealing with a person who from the outside appears normal? Sympathetic family and friends allowed me to whine and complain, but they had no more solutions to offer than I did. Some acquaintances that I felt comfortable enough to share the situation with seemed to look at me as if I were the villain in the piece. "Well, now, that's your mama, poor thing, I'm sure she can't help being the way she is" or "If that were my mama, I would do everything I could for her while she was still living." They meant well by their comments, but the words only added to my guilt, frustration, and angst. I kept thinking, *But you don't know what I'm dealing with, you don't see what I see every day.*

The mobile home was in disrepair; nobody was there to do routine maintenance inside. The clothes dryer quit working, so Mama started washing and drying some of her clothes at Mrs. Thibodeaux's house. My siblings and I held our breaths about how long Mama would be able to stay in the trailer alone.

Johnny did do some of the necessary repair work on the outside of the trailer. Once, he repaired the front deck when its cover started leaking into the front door right after Christmas. By late January, we were experiencing what we refer to as a false spring, a few days when the temperature climbs to the upper 60s or low 70s. Johnny asked a friend to help him do the repair work.

When he came home that afternoon, his friend was with him. They both expressed their disgust at the condition of the porch. Johnny shared with me that there were several boxes of food rotting on the porch floor. Our friend said he had never seen red worms in a pile of rotting food.

The next day I stopped by Mama's and saw what they had seen. Mama knew how to contact any service agency in the central Louisiana area that gave boxes of food to needy people prior to the Thanksgiving and Christmas holidays. There was no way to tell how many agencies Mama called, but judging by the waste on the porch, she had called more than one. The boxes had been sitting on the porch since before Christmas.

I wanted to cry when I saw the bags of flour and corn meal with their contents slowly seeping out and the canned goods rusted through with their contents gushing out the sides of the box. With a cast-off piece of wood, I poked around in the mess and saw the red worms for myself. It was disgusting and disheartening to see this waste.

The cellophane and shiny red bow that once encased the gift box of staple food, fruit, and nuts now dismally flapped in the breeze, mocking me. This sealed my shame and taunted me with the evidence of my mother's disregard of the generosity of strangers who had worked hard to gather food for those in real need. Mama wasn't needy, and she took advantage of and exploited others to feed her malignant greed. I came to empathize briefly with those who don't want to give to charitable causes because of people like my own mother.

Since she didn't go anywhere that required the need to dress up, for years Mama had only been wearing clothes she found comfortable. She had taken to wearing muumuus, sans brassiere, and rubber, slip-on shoes. She purchased material by the yard that caught her eye at garage sales or at the TG&Y. Mama then took sacks of the drably colored material, mostly heavy-weight fabrics, to our family friend

Mynette, who is a seamstress. Mynette made the sleeveless sack dresses for Mama, charging her only a nominal fee because she was kind—but Mama wore very few of the dresses our friend had made. Later, we found bags of the finished garments scattered about the mobile home.

One particular muumuu was made of thick material and patterned with a small forest-green-and-black plaid, which Mama seemed to wear continuously. When I picked her up to go on one of her necessary excursions, my car would fill with the primal odor of oniony-smelling sweat and stale tobacco. Mama had stopped shaving her legs and underarms years before, and it was apparent that she wasn't bathing with any regularity. Flakes of dandruff drifted down from her short, dark, slicked-back hair onto her neck and shoulders. Her once-beautiful large white teeth had all been pulled, but she never wore the sets of dentures paid for with Medicaid funds.

During this time, Janis and I began to discuss seriously the state of Mama's mental health. We still had not heard from any clinician exactly what her diagnosis was, although she continued to go to the mental health clinic for medication. I started hearing and reading things about obsessive-compulsive disorder and other mental health problems. Janis found some information about obsessive-compulsive hoarding and sent me a copy. The information fit Mama's behavior.

One of the difficulties I had when Daddy was sick was that Mama had not once considered getting rid of things so that Daddy could come home to die. Her selfishness haunted me and thoroughly pissed me off. I couldn't hide how I felt in conversations with Janis.

My first glimmer of recognition about the dynamics of the disorder came when Janis said that, according to what she had been reading, for someone with the disorder, losing their things was more painful than losing someone they were supposed to love. I understood that intellectually, but emotionally I struggled. I started researching the disorder.

Life didn't stop just because I knew a little more about OCD. I was too emotionally bound to the unhealthy relationship I had with Mama. I remember driving Mama into Alexandria for one of her monthly mental-health group therapy days. It was frustrating to me that she only went to get her medication. The social worker would beg her to stay, to take part in the little therapeutic art projects, and to socialize with the other outpatients. Mama was good at lying; often she used one of her grandchildren or me as her excuse for not being able to stay.

On the way home, I asked her why she didn't take part in the groups. Her reply was that she didn't want "to fool with them old crazy people." As I drove home in silence on that gray winter day, and as I approached a curve in the Pineville expressway, I thought about how easy it would be not to maintain the curve and to drive us straight into the dark-green pine trees. It occurred to me that would never work—with my luck I'd be killed and she would walk away, unscathed.

Mama was isolating inside the mobile home more and more. She didn't want anyone to come in, even me. That old, dark secret continued to monopolize her lonely existence.

I vividly remember Mama's need to keep her secret life from others. She called me in a panic one Sunday just as I was preparing to take my children to an afternoon movie. She called from Mrs. Thibodeaux's house because her telephone wasn't working. She almost begged me to come see what was wrong with it.

It was useless to tell her to call the phone company because she knew they might need to come inside. I told her I would come before we left for the movie. She begged me to please hurry. By then every situation was dramatic and an emergency. And I was the one who had to handle these so-called dilemmas.

I stopped by and parked in her driveway, leaving the kids in the van because they didn't like to go to their grandmother's house. I hadn't been in the trailer (as we refer to mobile homes in the South) for a few months, mainly because she wouldn't let me in. She always greeted me on the front porch. Sometimes, she would motion for me to come across the road to Mrs. Thibodeaux's house, where she spent most of her time.

As I entered the trailer, she talked incessantly. She jabbered about how the phone wasn't working and that it must be the cord. She desperately needed me to "see about it" because she had to have her phone. The talk was meant to deflect my attention from what I was about to see. Immediately, I tensed up because the mountains were enormous and the darkness and the smell in the trailer were oppressive.

She had a black, desk phone perched on the arm of the only chair she could sit in. A cord hung from the phone, which was probably one of the longest you could buy. I went to the phone, picked up the cord, and started trying to trace it to its jack. Mama was decidedly nervous, because she knew that I was going to have to go down her hall and into her bedroom to find the jack.

Before I could get out of the living room, I felt my father's energy come over me, and I erupted with a verbal tirade she had not heard for a while.

All I could think to say was, "What in the hell are you doing living this way? Do you realize that one fucking spark in here would burn you alive before you could get out the door? The fire marshal would condemn this place in a New York minute and you would have nowhere to live if they ever came in here. One spark and this whole place would go up in a flash, and there would be no way for you to get out!"

I ranted and raved for a full five minutes because I was so angry and frustrated. All the while she was patting me on the arm, saying, "It's okay, baby, it's okay. Mama needs her phone and I'll clean it up as soon as I can."

My aggravation only worsened as I made my way down the narrow hallway. The feelings I had were similar to flashbacks suffered by those diagnosed with posttraumatic stress disorder—I was reliving my childhood and I was mad as hell at the impotent way I was feeling.

Once in the hallway, I had to squeeze by two chests of drawers she had somehow wedged into that narrow space. The short distance to her bedroom seemed miles long because I had to physically twist and turn to maneuver into her bedroom. I could feel my face flush and I felt hot, although the trailer was not heated that day. Had I been the least bit claustrophobic I wouldn't have been able to go further.

The sight of the bedroom appalled me. Mama had pushed the king-size bed against the outer wall; four feet of blankets insulated the bed, rendering it useless. Large, bulging black plastic garbage bags and miscellaneous clothes filled the room, shrouding the window at the far end. The pile of fabric and plastic cast a foreboding gloom over everything. It became difficult to distinguish where one thing began and another ended.

As my eyes adjusted to the dim light, I noticed an indented space close to the outside edge of the mattress. It became obvious to me that this was where she was sleeping. I was horrified. She was actually occupying a space no more than two feet or three feet wide so that she could continue to pile more things on the bed. The indention was well worn and nasty. The pillow and sheet were foul and dingy from her sweat and body grime. I was overwhelmed, speechless.

I believe she sensed this overwhelming sickness I was feeling. This is the kind of sickness that has your soul in a vice-grip; one that I didn't think I could ever shake loose. I glanced her way with a kind of loathing.

She quickly encouraged me on to find the telephone jack. I resignedly turned to face another damn chest, which I had to pull away from the wall while still maintaining sight of the telephone cord.

She reached out to give me a hand by holding the chest away from the wall. I was not appreciative. I looked at her with such a look of scorn that I was surprised she didn't hit me. My anger intensified as I squatted to reach behind the chest with the cord in my right hand.

When I squatted down next to several garbage bags on the floor, the underside of my left thigh rested slightly on a bag. No sooner had I gotten my balance, than something vibrated against my leg. My immediate thought was that it was some kind of snake in the bag!

I screamed, and with all my might, I hurled the offensive chest out of my way. I saw the wall jack and the disconnected cord. I plugged it back in quicker than I had ever done anything in my life! My only desire was to exit that life-sucking room and that trailer and Mama immediately.

As I made my way back through the maze and toward the door, she was calling after me, thanking me for fixing her phone. She added a few manipulative phrases (in order to make me feel guilty) about how she didn't want to be without a phone in case she got sick and needed to call somebody.

At that moment, I could not have cared less. I stormed out of the mobile home. I could only shake my head and bite my tongue as I approached the van with my waiting children. I never wanted to have to deal with her again. Inside I was screaming, *I want a way out, a way out!* All I knew to do was to go on with my life, fully knowing that the next time she called, I would be there.

From then on, Mama kept me at arm's length so that I wouldn't see the condition of the mobile home, but honestly, I didn't want to know how bad it was. After the phone incident with the rattling garbage bag, I never wanted to step foot in the place again. In my rational moments, however, I knew I was on borrowed time before something drastic occurred.

The reality of how dangerously she was living slapped me upside the head one late afternoon in April 1994. I decided to take some fried fish over to her, one of her favorite meals. When I drove into the driveway, I expected to see her come out and greet me on the small wooden deck of the mobile home. When she didn't come out, I looked toward Mrs. Thibodeaux's house, expecting to see Mama emerge from Estelle's living room. I didn't see her.

By the time I got out of the car, I was beginning to get anxious that something had happened. I made my way through the yard, weaving around the porta-potties, crutches, and other equipment she had conned from some helping institution. This expensive equipment, given to Mama by way of taxpayer dollars, was now the place where weeds, snails, and other creatures made their home.

I got up onto the deck and opened the door. The place was dark even though there was still plenty of daylight left. I didn't want to step all the way in. The air inside the mobile home was fetid. It reeked of rotting food, dust, roaches, and human shit.

I swallowed hard, half expecting to find her dead in her chair. I peered cautiously around the mound of clothes. My eyes adjusted to the light, and then I saw her sitting in the far corner of the living room.

The hair on the back of my arms stood up. I wasn't sure then and am certainly not sure now what I was witnessing. The air was malevolent. In that one brief moment, before she knew I was there, I saw a complete look of contentment on her raised face. She was staring mindlessly in the air, slowly rubbing her arms.

A thought flashed through my mind, startling me into breaking the silence. It was hard for me to dispel the image forming in my mind of a black widow. That picture was burning behind my eyes. I called out, but it took my mother a few moments to realize fully that I was in the mobile home.

I quickly brought us both back to reality by rushing through the debris on the floor and pushing the plate of fish into her lap. Her excitement over the food kept her from focusing on my presence in her space. I made some excuse for having to leave hurriedly. She was calling out her thanks to me as I fled.

A week or so later, the dire circumstances under which she lived came to my attention one more time. I could no longer flee. She had been calling me almost daily with one crisis after another. She routinely demanded that I take her to the Huey P. Long Hospital emergency room for feigned illnesses or to the grocery store or to some other made-up place of importance. These demands were becoming her way of controlling my life.

That afternoon she came quickly out of the mobile home because she knew how irritated I was when she called me at my shop, earlier, about needing to go to the hospital. She stepped off the deck steps, tossed her cigarette out into the yard, bent down, and quickly pulled something out of the sole of the rubber flip-flops she wore year-round.

My irritation turned to outrage when I saw that she had pulled a used syringe from her shoe and then casually tossed it up against the metal wall of the mobile home. It fell into the grass alongside the metal skirting.

Patrick had been coming weekly to mow her yard with a push mower. Her disregard for someone else's safety, tossing her insulin syringes wherever she pleased, could impact the well-being of my child. I was livid.

It had come down to knowing that I was going to have to do something to place her where she could be monitored. I just didn't know what direction to go. At the time, I couldn't catch a break. I had three children in school, a disabled husband, and a small floral business that was barely hanging on. And Mama was calling me daily.

I talked to Janis and Kitty (who were still living in Texas at the time) and Oscar about what their thoughts were. They all agreed that something had to be done, but like me, they couldn't think of any reasonable solutions. None of us could consider bringing her into our homes.

I checked into having her legally interdicted. I didn't know if I wanted the legal responsibility or could afford the legal expense of having her rights taken from her. It was also indicated to me that I would have to prove her incompetence. Someone told me from legal aid that if she knew what day it was, could self-administer medication, and could self-feed, I would have a hard time proving incompetence. I felt stuck in the mire.

That hypervigilant state was overwhelming me. She called me at eleven o'clock one morning saying that she was having chest pains and was short of breath. I told her I couldn't just leave my place of business in the middle of the day and that she should call an ambulance.

Immediately, she started whining about the expense of an ambulance and that she didn't have anyone else and she needed to go right away. I knew that this was another false alarm. She was crying wolf, but I felt compelled to go. "Miss Responsibility of the Century" would not be able to live with herself if Mama died because she didn't go.

She was waiting for me at the end of the driveway. I fumed the whole way to the emergency room. This time, instead of leaving her at the door, I went in with her. She didn't want me there. I told her whether she liked it or not I was staying.

I wanted to find out what, if anything, was wrong with her. I barged my way into conversations with anyone who saw her. My presence and outspoken demeanor got results. I soon learned that the hospital personnel were tired of dealing with her. She had become one of the regulars they often saw. They decided quickly that they would send her to the mental health facility across the river in Alexandria. She was taken by ambulance. She was not happy.

Once there, she was seen by a new psychiatrist who had not previously seen her during her regular monthly visits. She hadn't actually seen a psychiatrist there for a while, through no fault of theirs. She dodged having to see anyone by making up excuses. Mama had played the personnel with one song and dance or another; she would get her monthly meds and leave.

I parked myself right next to her and waited for the doctor. Mama told me I could go on; she knew that I had stuff to do. I told her it was okay; I was staying. She didn't look pleased. When the doctor came in she began to tell him she had just been feeling a little bad, that maybe she was congested and that she would be okay if he gave her some medicine, she just wanted to go home.

I listened to Mama manipulate the doctor. I glanced alternately at the doctor and then at the ceiling. The small office seemed to get smaller, but the ceiling was getting higher. Her voice was calm and believable. My heart pounded in my throat. The doctor reached for his prescription pad. The white room appeared bright white. Before I knew what I was doing, I reacted.

I looked at the doctor and said, "No, you have to hear how she's been behaving." I proceeded not quite hysterically to fill him in on her demands and frequent trips to the emergency room and about how she was living. The entire time I spoke, Mama slapped her hand on my thigh, telling me to hush. She peppered my plea to the doctor with threats, denials, and reassurances that she was okay.

Later, I was surprised that I wasn't taken to another room for my own mental health examination. But the doctor saw something in my eyes or heard something in my voice that told him our situation had become dire. He asked a few pointed questions. Although Mama was insistent that she be allowed to go home, he decided that she needed to go to a local mental health facility for a few days.

I felt ready to collapse from sheer relief. The kicker of it was that I had to transport Mama there. I figured that drive might be my last, but she surprised me by staying relatively calm. She did admonish me about leaving her stuff alone in the mobile home—I felt that creepy sense of wondering if she had some kind of weird, psychic ability to know what I had been thinking.

A whirlwind of events occurred once Mama was in the facility. I got to know the social worker, Rena Powell, very well. She listened intently to my concerns and beliefs about Mama being an obsessive-compulsive hoarder. She was open to looking at the Polaroid snapshots of the interior of the mobile home that I had taken.

I finally had someone who was in my corner, someone who was willing to listen and willing to go the extra steps necessary to move the process forward. Rena treated Mama with respect. She wasn't swayed by Mama's manipulation and was able to gain her trust.

I made repeated attempts to get Mama to go into a nursing home, but she stubbornly refused. I felt under the gun because I had a limited amount of time to prove my case. I couldn't risk the chance of her being released and wanting to return home. I was convinced that if that were to happen I would eventually find her dead or receive a call that she had burned up in the mobile home.

Once she was away, I was able to get a better look at her living conditions. She was no longer cooking for herself. There was evidence that she had been eating out of cans. I couldn't walk through the kitchen; bags of garbage and boxes of rotting food blocked it. Mama had covered the counter tops with everything from red plastic cans of coffee, jars of peanut butter, other miscellaneous cans of opened food, glassware, pots, and pans stacked high. There appeared to be what seemed like yards and yards of diaphanous fabric, which in reality were spiderwebs.

The interior of my mother's mobile home, showing what greeted me as I entered her living room

Kitty's former bedroom

The living room

The obviously unusable bathroom

The kitchen with its diaphanous spiderwebs

The chair where my mother spent most of her time

The impenetrable kitchen

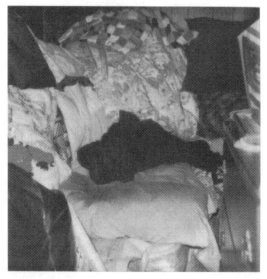

The king-size bed where my mother once slept

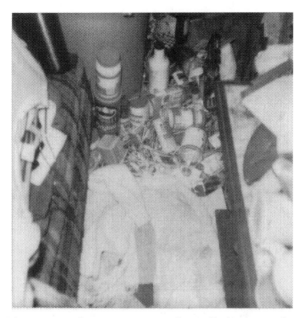

The spent insulin syringes my mother walked on every day.

On the floor, I saw a cardboard soda flat filled with something that looked like coffee grounds or the remains of a cake that had disintegrated into a mysterious black mound. As I stood staring incredulously at this frightening scene, I thought of how my son, Patrick, referred to Mama as a shape-shifter. That was the only way he or any of us could imagine how she was able to maneuver around all this stuff without burying herself alive.

In the living room, spent syringes lined the pathway she walked along every day. Her diabetes had spiraled out of control and it had become necessary for her to take two shots of insulin each day. The boxes of chocolate-covered cherries stacked two deep next to her chair were obviously compounding that issue. A large, gray plastic garbage can stood guard next to her chair; syringes and empty cigarette packs spilled out when I attempted to pass by it.

The chair Daddy used to sit in had now become her chair; it was darkened and stained by urine and sweat. It horrified and saddened me to think that she had been sleeping in that chair. I was even more convinced of that when I saw a wadded-up bath towel with evidence of mucus and feces. An oversized flashlight was perched on the chair arm.

The bathroom looked as if it had not been used in a long time. The tub was filled with garbage cans stuffed with sheets, blankets, and towels. The blackened, crusted rim and interior of the commode indicated to me that she wasn't using it either.

Mama had confined herself to living in that one corner of the living room. Other than going to Mrs. Thibodeaux's home in the late afternoons, where she had been sharing a cooked meal, she had isolated herself from all human contact. I now realized that her jaunts to the emergency room had become some kind of outing or break from the overwhelming chaos of her existence.

I got my daughter's boyfriend, Shawn, to make a video of the interior of the mobile home. It was risky asking anyone to try and negotiate the mobile home because there were so many hazards hampering movement. I felt I needed as much evidence as I could get to back up my concerns about Mama remaining in the mobile home.

The next step I took was to ask the mayor of Ball and an official of the health department to come have a look at Mama's living conditions. I felt it necessary to have someone in an official capacity see how my mother was living so that it did not appear that I was making false statements. I was up against manipulative powers that had defeated me before.

Mayor Roy Hebron kindly agreed to help me out. He brought a sanitation employee and the chief of police with him as backup. We all met at the mobile home. I opened the door and invited them in, but Mayor Hebron and the health department official declined. Once they stuck their heads in the door, they thought it wasn't safe to enter.

The sanitation employee and the chief said that it didn't bother them. The three of us managed to push and shove our way into all the rooms. The men came out shaking their heads, declaring that it was hard to imagine how anyone could live there. The health department official told me that if we chose to clean the mobile home out, we would have to dispose of the syringes properly by placing them into plastic containers. He said that we couldn't simply throw them into the trash.

I continued to work on Mama. She continued to refuse. I believe she knew I was up to something. Rena listened empathetically to my fears and frustrations and continued to work on Mama as well. Her stay in the facility had been extended from a few days to a month.

It looked more and more as if I might have to do the interdiction. Just as I was about to give up, Rena excitedly called one day to say that she had worked on Mama that morning by appealing to her sense of "What's in it for me?" Rena had made the case that Mama would benefit by having people look out for her and help her with everything. Mama had finally agreed! That seemed like a huge victory.

Within months of entering the nursing home, Mama's diabetes was under control. She no longer had to have insulin injections; an oral medication replaced them. With controlled portions at mealtime, she lost some weight; her color and overall health was better.

When I went to see her, she still bitterly complained about her stuff. She kept asking about what I had done with the mobile home. I knew her expectation was that the mobile home was to stay just as she left it. I avoided answering her questions as much as I could. I didn't want her to know that Johnny had shoveled everything out of the trailer and burned it. I refused to have anything to do with the disposal of all that stuff.

The overall situation with Mama was better. I felt some relief, but the problem of hoarding didn't go away. While the medical staff who attended to Mama recognized what her problem was, there was no therapy given to her to address her hoarding issues.

Even in the nursing home, she managed to hoard. Within six months of her placement, the director was calling me to say that I needed to come and remove some of the belongings Mama had collected. This went on for more than a year. It wasn't as frustrating as before because the staff would bag or box the items, they weren't dirty or moldy, and I could dispose of them relatively easily by donating them to a charitable organization.

I moved Mama to a nursing home closer to my home. She didn't like the idea at first but soon adjusted. The pattern continued there. It was frustrating to see how Mama's hoarding was affecting the way the nursing home staff had to deal with her. They couldn't readily have her share a room with another woman because Mama would usurp that person's space by filling it up or by pilfering their belongings. Mama had numerous roommates before she was eventually left alone in the room. She then had double the space to acquire more things.

The year 1999 was an eventful year in my life. Courtney and Shawn married in April. I helped her plan her wedding and worked hard to give her the wedding she so deserved. St. Michael's was overflowing with friends and family who came to be a part of the beautiful ceremony. My daughter was a stunningly beautiful bride.

At the end of May, I left Johnny after twenty-seven years of marriage. I filed for divorce in November, after years of struggle. I had believed in the bond of marriage—my father taught me that.

A few months after leaving Johnny, I got a nasty call from Mama. Her powers of detection had been hard at work, allowing her to find my new phone number. She promptly told me that she knew I had left Johnny and the kids, had bought a fancy, red car, and was living in a fancy, expensive apartment.

As I sat on the floor of my tiny kitchen, listening to her hurtful words, knowing it would be of little use to offer an explanation, listening to her stretch the truthful part of her accusations into her own weird version of reality, I briefly felt guilt. Her artful skills at manipulation were working once again.

When I didn't immediately react to her nastiness, she began to tell me what a bad daughter I was. She heaped on me that I didn't care anything about her, hadn't been to see her, and hadn't done anything for her lately. I allowed her to spew her venom for about five minutes.

During that time, I thought of my fourteen-year-old daughter, Colleen, asleep on the other side of the apartment. I thought of how I had gone back to school after a twenty-year gap to finish my bachelor's degree, how I had been working a full-time job as a counselor of battered women, worked a part-time job in retail, and designed flowers for every wedding I could get. Mama didn't know that the "fancy red car" was a reconditioned Taurus a friend had sold me for very little or that I had also taken the responsibility of a second mortgage Johnny and I shared.

I sat stoically and thought of all the times I had tried to tell Mama no. I thought of all the times she had manipulated me and how I let myself feel guilty about her and responsible for her. I thought about how she didn't listen to any of my requests and how each time she failed to honor me as a person, she took a little more of my power away from me. I also thought about the advice my social worker friend had given me years before: run like hell.

I stared at the ceiling with her words pounding in my ear. A grace-filled epiphany occurred. I knew what I had to do. I knew it was time to let go. Mama wasn't going to change her behavior; she was resistant to change. I, on the other hand, was on the verge of hate. If I allowed myself to slip down into that darkness then I would be lost—I would be damaging myself.

Calmly, when she stopped ranting, I said, "You're right, Mama. I left Johnny, but when I looked fifteen minutes ago, Colleen was asleep in her bed. Courtney and Patrick are grown. I am going to divorce Johnny, and by the way, I'm divorcing you too."

She replied, "What do you mean?"

I said, "Exactly what you think I mean. I'm done, finished. This is the last time I will listen to you tell me what a bad wife, a bad mother, and a bad daughter I am. Take care, Mama. Bye."

I didn't speak to my mother again until five years later. It was Sunday, August 28, 2005, the day before Hurricane Katrina hit New Orleans. By that time, I had remarried a kind and gentle-spirited man. I met Ken at St. Michael's—both of us had come out of long-term marriages seeking a little peace in our lives.

The very air that day held a deep, foreboding feeling. It was unusual for me to have missed church and to be home on a Sunday morning. When I saw the nursing home name come up on Caller ID, I thought perhaps someone was calling me to say that Mama had died.

I was uneasy answering the phone, but then I heard her voice. It was as though five years simply melted away. As soon as she heard my voice, she spoke as if she had talked to me the day before.

In a stern, rough tone she told me she wanted her stuff back, she knew Johnny had her rings, jewelry, and all her pictures. I thought how odd it was for her to bring up Johnny. He had cleared the mobile home out after Mama went into the nursing home. Mama had managed to find that out somehow, but that incident had occurred six years before.

Mama demanded that I bring her things to her immediately. I briefly explained to her that I didn't know where her stuff was, but that if I talked to Johnny, I would let him know. I didn't tell her that all those things had been long gone; it would have been of no use to dredge up that kind of old business. I managed to end the conversation quickly.

Her call rattled me. It was so random and unexpected and so eerily curious. For the rest of that day my soul felt disturbed. In desperation, I called my friend Midori, a nurse who is of Japanese descent. I knew she could help me sort through my feelings.

From her Asian perspective, she convinced me that my mother was reaching out to me. She thought that quite possibly, she was sinking deeper into her mental illness or that possibly she was in the process of dying. Midori's words haunted me the rest of the day.

I knew I would have to see Mama. I also knew that I wasn't going to go alone. I asked my friend Father George Gennuso and St. Michael's Deacon Belle Rollins (who had been a social worker) to accompany me. Graciously, they both agreed.

I had no idea what to expect when we got to the nursing home. The visit was as odd as the phone conversation. Mama acted as though no time had elapsed. She said nothing about the previous five years.

Mama sat, confined to a wheelchair by her own doing. I learned later that she had repeatedly demanded one. The therapy aid put Mama's endless requests for a wheelchair off as long as he could until she eventually wore him down. He said he knew that once she got the chair her health would go downhill.

I didn't expect to see Mama with long hair; she habitually wore it cut short. When I asked why she was wearing it long and pinned up, she told me that Daddy always wanted her to have long hair. That statement seemed so bizarre to me, I couldn't forget it. As with the wheelchair, I later learned that she had been so belligerent and demanding when she went to the nursing home beauty shop, they banned her from coming back.

She sported several rings on both hands and a nice pair of dangling earrings. Her explanation for the jewelry was that Janis had bought it for her. I doubted the truth of that, except for the earrings. I was to discover that quite possibly my mother had stolen the rings from other residents or staff.

Perhaps the saddest part of the visit was to witness the fact that she could no longer see. The diabetes had taken her sight. Watching her so stiff in the wheelchair, except for a slight positioning of her head toward whoever spoke, made me feel exceedingly sad. I was also left with the impression that she inhabited a world of her own choosing.

Other than a strong wash of sadness, I felt no other particular emotions. The visit had been uneventful. Mama was quite talkative about mundane things, putting her best foot forward to charm Father George and Deacon Belle.

After the visit, they asked me how I felt. I was in an odd place. My feelings came from what I observed. I felt as though I had seen a cracked vessel. Whatever my former perception of Mama's essence might have been, it now seemed to be slipping away. Whatever had controlled and driven her for so many years was letting her go. It had used her up. I felt that once it was gone all that would be left would be a badly cracked, empty vessel.

I saw Mama one last time a few weeks later. Kitty, Oscar, and I went to visit her on a Sunday afternoon. She answered some questions we had about the past. She seemed most comfortable keeping the conversation centered on long-ago people and events. We seemed to annoy her if we didn't particularly remember certain people or incidences. The visit was fairly lighthearted and uneventful. We left with promises of visiting again.

The three of us slipped back into our regular routines, time slipped away without us fulfilling our promise. Janis called to let us know when Mama was admitted to the hospital at various times for the next year or so. I didn't choose to go visit her; I suppose I was reminded of all the times before when she unnecessarily cried wolf.

I felt only mild regret that I hadn't seen her again when she died two years later, oddly enough, on August 28, 2007. My son, Patrick, accompanied me to the hospital when Janis called. Kitty met us, as did Mama's brother, Uncle Robert, and his wife, Sandra. Janis waited for us outside and then took us to the emergency room where Mama lay.

Janis had picked up the mantle of responsibility for Mama after I bailed. She had been seeing to Mama's needs. She handled the funeral arrangements.

I thought it fitting that she ended the service at Hixson Brothers' Funeral Home in Pineville with the playing of Fats Domino's song, "Walking to New Orleans." Of those few who attended, mostly members of Daddy's family, some of Mama's family, and our close friends, no one realized the significance of the song.

All four of us kids were quietly overcome with emotion as the words of the song echoed through the funeral home. I glanced around and saw Marbeth, Frog, Uncle Robert, and Uncle Earl. They sat with traces of smiles, nodding their heads in time to the music.

We children were remembering Mama in her younger days, as I'm sure they were remembering a young Christine. We were able to remember the young woman who briefly appeared to have had joy in her life when she listened to Fats and shuffled her feet in flat shoes and then bounced across the floor in time to the music.

Nevertheless, I mostly remembered a woman who seemed never to have had an opportunity to reach fulfillment because she was never satisfied. I felt that she would not allow herself to be fulfilled by engaging in personal connections because any opportunity to do so was superseded by her connection to things. My mother was a woman-child who was not capable enough or motivated enough to reach out and grab a chance to know her full potential. She never let anyone near the dark place she internally inhabited. I carry with me that enduring sadness.

Was she the way she was because of an odd quirk in her DNA? Or had things transpired the way they did because of the environment in which she was raised? Or was it a combination of those things? No matter how much I've tried to analyze the situation, no answer reveals itself. To think that she was mentally ill and to leave it there suffices for a time.

Chapter 18

Remaining True to Myself

The haunting aspect of having grown up in the presence of a mother who was abusive was difficult enough in itself. However, that coupled with her also being an obsessive-compulsive hoarder compounded the difficulties in our relationship. I was never afforded an opportunity to know who my mother was. She never revealed aspirations, dreams, or desires that might have given me an inkling of her humanity. It is sad and unfortunate that for most of my life I demonized the woman who gave birth to me. Her behavior and attitudes frightened me.

I spent years trying to take care of my mother, to be a dutiful daughter, to be in a relationship, but it was one-sided and extremely unhealthy. In essence, the roles shifted; I became the parent and she the child.

We were locked in a perpetual tug-of-war played out on an emotional battlefield where I was always the loser. I could not satisfy her childlike desires to have situations go her way. The demands were huge; nothing was too extreme to ask. She lacked consideration toward the needs and lives of anyone else.

I could not see this while thus engaged, much like not being able to see the forest for the trees. Once I allowed myself distance, I was better able to gain a more realistic perspective on the dynamics of Mama's illness. Then and only then was I able to gain a sense of empathy for a woman who spent a lifetime as a wounded child. I had to accept that my mother was a woman who was robbed of the joy of being in relationship to others instead of self.

The anger and frustration subsided because I was no longer bound to the day-to-day "ninny-nannies" (as I refer to them), which could be maddening to overcome as I dealt with Mama and her obsessive-compulsive disorder. I stopped unconsciously colluding with the disease. So much time is wasted in trying to satisfy, placate, or understand the idiosyncrasies someone possesses in association with OCD.

In trying to make sense of it, I fell victim to "if only": If only Mama would stop collecting unnecessary stuff, if only Mama could be like other mothers, if only Mama weren't so greedy, if only Mama could show me some genuine affection, if only Mama would bathe (the list was endless), then I might feel as though I was like everyone else.

I could stop living in the storybook world where real moms treated their children with tenderness and understanding, baked cookies with them for school events, and later shared in the birth of a grandchild or just simply went to lunch on a nice spring day without embarrassment or conflict. That fictional world is not the reality of the child of someone with OCD. Unfortunately, many friends or well-intentioned family members complicate the already complicated mess of OCD with this sort of wishful thinking.

The time and energy necessary to attend to Mama's needs and demands left me absolutely drained. Being robbed of energy and motivation left me feeling trapped in a vicious cycle. I began feeling as if I just wanted to get the crisis of a particular day finished. I knew no way to reach a middle ground with my own mother or to reach constructive outcomes.

Whatever the crisis might have been, it got in the way—bogged me down, so that I was not actually ever able to face the illness head on. I began hoping that each new episode with her would be the last one and that things would get better. The brief respites, however, also would sink me further into denial and, therefore, further away from finding concrete answers and help.

What my family and I once thought of as the most shameful family secret one could imagine has now emerged as something many people have experienced. Current statistics state that over three million individuals are obsessive-compulsive hoarders.

For us, too many years had to pass with that secret intact because we didn't know it wasn't an unusual occurrence. During my childhood, there was no manual, self-help book, or local group to offer support to my family or me. We didn't know where to find help or even how to reach out for help. We felt that it was a family issue and that our family needed to deal with it.

I have written about my experiences with my mother's mental health issues as part of my personal journey to understand the disorder a little better. In chronicling these experiences, I had to become brutally honest about my feelings in a way that did not portray me as another victim of a dysfunctional family. By remaining true to myself, I gained a sense of purpose. I saw before me an opportunity to take elements from my ordinary story and weave them together so that some other ordinary person like me might gain insight and, perhaps, hope.

I pursued a deliberate path to enlighten myself in order to rid myself of the overwhelming feeling that my mother cared more about things than she did about my sisters, my brother, my father, and me. I struggled to come to a place where I could feel a degree of empathy and understanding for my mother in order to strengthen my enlightenment.

The years it has taken to get the story on paper have been a gut-wrenching, soul-searching, tears—and snot-producing experience of reliving those turbulent times. Although this process has been extraordinarily painful, it has also been liberating. If in sharing my experiences I can help someone else see that he deserves a measure of peace and release from pain, then it has been worth the effort.

The public needs an opportunity to understand that obsessive-compulsive hoarding is not just another tragedy affecting someone else, nor does it give one a scintillating excuse to rubberneck voyeuristically.

The disorder also does not provide grounds for unwarranted judgment toward the sufferer. Open, honest dialogue about the disorder is the key to change. Hoarding is detrimental not only to the hoarder and to that person's family, but to the community at large. The increased risk of fire and insect, rodent, and other creature infestation ultimately affects everyone.

I have learned that the painful times of life can be far less painful if we reach out to others, allowing them an opportunity to help us along the way. A good place to start is with local mental health care providers who can offer information, support, or a treatment plan. There are more resources available now and more current information about obsessive-compulsive hoarding and about parental abuse than ever before. No longer do individuals or families have to contemplate facing these issues alone.

Included is a resource section with national contact information for organizations dealing with hoarding, mental health, and child abuse.

Resources

Organizations on Hoarding:

International OCD Foundation
1-617-973-5801
http://www.ocfoundation.org

NAMI—National Alliance on Mental Illness
1-800-950-NAMI
http://www.nami.org

Books about Hoarding:

Randy O. Frost, PhD; and Gail S. Steketee, PhD.
Stuff: Compulsive Hoarding and the Meaning of Things.
New York, New York: Houghton Mifflin Harcourt
    Publishing Company, 2010.

Fugen Neziroglu, PhD, ABPP; Jerome Bubrick, PhD; and
    Jose Yaryura-Tobias, MD.
Overcoming Compulsive Hoarding.
Oakland, CA: New Harbinger Publications, 2004.

David F. Tolin, PhD; Randy O. Frost, PhD; and Gail S.
    Steketee, PhD.
*Buried in Treasures: Help for Compulsive Acquiring, Saving,
    and Hoarding.*
New York, New York: Oxford University Press, Inc., 2007.

Michael A. Tompkins, PhD; and Tamara L. Hartl, PhD.
*Digging Out: Helping Your Loved One Manage Clutter,
    Hoarding, and Compulsive*
Acquiring.
Oakland, CA: Harbinger Publications, 2009.

Child Abuse Resources:

Childhelp—Prevention and Treatment of Child
Abuse Hotline 1-800-4-A-Child
http://www.childhelp.org

National Children's Alliance
1-800-239-9950
http://www.nationalchildrensalliance.org